THROUGH GREEK EYES

Frontispiece: *Poseidon, god of the sea. The sculptor has tried to show the power and majesty of the god. Originally the statue had eyes of stone or clay.*

THROUGH GREEK EYES

Greek civilisation in the words of Greek writers

compiled, translated and introduced by

ROGER NICHOLS and KENNETH McLEISH

CAMBRIDGE UNIVERSITY PRESS

Published by the Syndics of the Cambridge University Press
Bentley House, 200 Euston Road, London NW1 2DB
American Branch: 32 East 57th Street, New York, N.Y. 10022

© *Cambridge University Press 1974*

Library of Congress Catalogue Card No. 74-80353

ISBN 0 521 08560 8

First published 1974

Photoset and Printed in Malta by St Paul's Press Ltd

Book designed by Peter Ducker
Maps and diagram p. 38 by Leslie Marshall

Contents

Artemis, the archer-goddess. She was the sister of Apollo, and her special responsibilities included the moon, hunting and childbirth.

Note: On the subject of Greek proper names, we have followed a general policy of transliterating as exactly as possible. Where, however, the English form of a name is really well known (Homer, Oedipus, Delphi), we abandoned our principles and retained it.

Acknowledgments

Thanks are due to the following for permission to reproduce photographs: Mansell, pp. ii, 4, 26, 32, 36, 65, 88, 92, 105, 109, 112, 113, 116, 126; The Louvre, pp. v, 4, 12, 55, 60; German Archaeological Institute, Athens, pp. x, 10, 101; Elsevier, pp. 2, 5, 7, 18, 25, 37, 99, 108, 110, 120, 123; American School of Classical Studies, Agora Excavations, pp. 8, 29, 32; Phaidon Press Ltd, p. 12; Staatliche Antikenssammlung, Munich, pp. 15, 41, 102; The British Museum, pp. 17, 23, 27, 35, 48, 49, 63, 71, 73, 74, 98; Batsford, pp. 19, 20, 60, 95; Courtesy of the Dumbarton Collection, Washington, D.C., p. 21; National Museum, Copenhagen, pp. 28, 66; Bibliothèque Nationale, Paris, pp. 29, 45; Metropolitan Museum of Art, New York, pp. 42, 58, 67, 70, 77, 78; Lionel Casson, p. 46; National Tourist Organisation of Greece, p. 51; Schools Council Publications, p. 52; Hirmer, pp. 56, 68, 97; Courtesy Museum of Fine Arts, Boston, p. 59; Taranto Museum, pp. 60, 64; Ashmolean Museum, Oxford, p. 69; The Vatican Museum, pp. 72, 86, 106, 112; Archaeological Museum, Florence, p. 104; Archaeological Museum, Olympia, p. 111; Archaeological Museum, Bologna, p. 127; Dayton, p. 134; Magnum Photos, p. 85; Greek Ministry of Culture, p. 85; A. F. Ketsting, p. 81; Eds. J. E. Bulloz, p. 83

to SARAH and VALERIE

Right: *The principal towns of Greece;*
Opposite: *The whole Greek world.*

N

SCYTHIA

R. Danube

BLACK SEA

Marseilles

A D R I A T I C   S E A

ITALY

CORSICA

Rome

SARDINIA   Cumae Naples

THRACE

MACEDON

Bosphorus

TO
Persian
Empire ▷

Hellespont
Troy

ASIA MINOR

SICILY   Messana

Athens

Syracuse

Sparta   Delos   Kos

To the
Pillars of
Herakles
(Straits
of Gibraltar)

A E G E A N   S E A

CRETE

CYPRUS

PHOENICIA
SYRIA

M E D I T E R R A N E A N   S E A

Alexandria

0   100 200 300 400 500 600 700 800 Km

EGYPT

R. Nile

ARABIA

RED SEA

ix

Bronze griffin's head, from Olympia.
Griffins were half eagles, half lions,
and were often shown in temple-
sculptures before 500 B.C.

1 · War

THE PLACE: Troy   THE TIME: c. 1190 B.C.

Just as reapers, standing opposite each other, cut swathes of wheat and barley
in the fields of some rich landowner, making the thick handfuls fall; so Trojans
and Greeks leapt on each other and began to fight. Fear was a stranger to them
and throughout the morning, as the sun grew brighter, the missiles of both
sides hit their mark and men fell. But about the hour when the woodcutter
prepares his supper in the mountain glens after a good day's work cutting the
tall trees and, feeling pleased with himself, begins to think about food, then it
was that the courage of the Greeks broke the enemy ranks, and along the line
they began to shout encouragement to their friends.

First, Agamemnon rushed forward and killed Bienor, one of the Trojan
leaders, and after him his friend Oileus, who was also his charioteer. He had
leapt down from the chariot and stood in Agamemnon's way, but for all his
eagerness to attack Agamemnon jabbed him in the forehead with his sharp
spear. Although the helmet was of heavy bronze, the spear went right through
it and through the bone, spattering his brains inside. That tamed his
enthusiasm. King Agamemnon left them there, their chests strangely white
after he had ripped off their tunics. Next he went to meet Isos and Antiphos,
two sons of Priam, who were both in the same chariot. Isos was driving, with
Antiphos at his side. The mighty Agamemnon struck Isos with his spear above
the nipple of his breast and caught Antiphos a fatal blow about the ear with
his sword, so that he toppled out of the chariot. Quickly, Agamemnon
stripped them of their fine armour. He was like a lion, which easily breaks
the necks of the young deer; going into their lair, he takes them in his strong
teeth and soon puts an end to their innocent lives. Their mother, even if she
happens to be close by, cannot help them. A terrible trembling shakes her
and swiftly she darts through the thick woods, through the undergrowth,
sweating in terror at the attack of the fearful beast. Just so, these two in the face
of death found no help from the Trojans; they too were in flight before the
Greeks.[1]

This was how later Greek schoolboys saw themselves in their own fights. Agamemnon, Ajax, Achilles: huge, bloodthirsty men, fighting private fights in any part of the battlefield they liked, not always too pleased at being called off to help somebody else. It was a primitive kind of war, in which brute force counted more than brains, and luck often more than either. But, by our standards, it was on a surprisingly small scale. Quite possibly, the total number engaged in the above battle was less than 1,000 men. The historian Thukydides, writing about seven centuries later, makes these comments:

It wasn't just that the Greeks didn't have the men, but more that they didn't have enough money to spend on supplies. So they took a relatively small army which could live off the land while it was fighting. At first, they won – they must have done, or else they wouldn't have been allowed to fortify their camp – but even after that they don't seem to have used the whole army at once. Instead, because they were still short of supplies, they spent a lot of their time growing food on the peninsula north of Troy and in plundering. It was because the Trojans only ever had to face a part of these scattered forces that they managed to hold out for as long as ten years.[2]

The scale of the fighting is also shown by the methods of description. No newspaper report of a modern battle would have room, and the reporter wouldn't think it necessary, to include accounts of single combat in such gruesome detail. By the time of the battle of Marathon in 490 B.C., fighting has become more a matter of tactics:

The Athenians had managed to cover the whole of the Persian front. Both wings were strong, but this had left the centre very thin.
When everything was ready and the sacrifices had turned out favourably, the word of command was given and the Athenians advanced at a run towards the enemy, who were at least a mile away. The Persians saw them coming at full tilt and prepared to resist; they were convinced that the Athenians must have gone mad, for such a small number to be rushing like this into the jaws of death, without even cavalry or archers to support them. That's what they thought. But as the fighting spread across the field of battle the Athenians fought a historic action. To the best of my knowledge, they were the first Greeks actually to run towards the enemy, and they were also the first not to be unmanned by the sight

Gold death-mask found at Mycenae. Schliemann, who discovered it, took it to be the death-mask of Agamemnon, who led the Greeks at Troy. It is now thought to belong to an earlier Mycenaean king.

3

Greek soldier. Notice his simple leather armour, and the long spear he carries (for use in the phalanx: *see page 9); and* right: *Persian soldier. He is armed with a spear, and a large quiver for arrows. He is wearing the robes of the Royal Guard.*

of the Persian armour and of the men inside. Until that day, just the word 'Persian' had been enough to send Greeks into a panic.

The fight at Marathon was a long one. The Persians and their allies in the centre were victorious, broke the Greek ranks opposite and chased them towards the hills. But on both wings the victory went to the Athenians and Plataians, who then let their Persian counterparts run away while they themselves swung inwards to meet and deal with the Persian centre which had broken through, so that the Athenians were victorious. The Persians fled and the Greeks gave chase, cutting them down until they reached the Persian ships, which they took hold of, shouting for firebrands. It was at this point that many

Aerial view of the plain of Marathon. The sea has receded some distance since the time of the battle; but even though the plain is now bigger, it is clear that with Greeks in front and mountains on three sides, the enemy would be easily trapped.

of the most outstanding Athenians were killed, including the chief-of-staff Kallimachos, a fine man, Stesilaos, one of the generals, and Kynegeiros, who grabbed the stern of a ship and had his hand chopped off with an axe. They overpowered seven ships like this, but the rest got away and sailed round Cape Sunion, with the idea of reaching Athens before the Athenian army could get back. But the Athenians, marching at top speed, got back to Athens first. When the Persian fleet finally arrived, it lay at anchor outside the main harbour of the city as if it meant to attack, but quite soon the ships sailed off back towards Asia Minor.

The numbers of the dead were: Persians 6,400; Athenians 192.[3]

Even if these casualty figures look suspiciously different, coming as they do from a Greek historian, Marathon was without doubt a brilliant victory, remembered proudly by generations of Athenians and a victory won without archers or cavalry. It was always the infantry, the so-called 'hoplites', heavily armed, that the Greeks relied on, and of these the most feared were the Spartans:

Xerxes sent a spy on horseback to see how many Greeks there were and what they were doing. The spy reached the camp and had a good look round. He couldn't see the whole army because some troops were out of sight behind the wall which they had repaired and put under guard, but he was able to observe those outside, whose weapons were lying around in front of the wall. At that moment these happened to be Spartans, some of whom were stripped as if for games, while others were combing their hair. The spy, very surprised, took all this in, counted their numbers, checked all possible details and then rode quietly away. He was not followed. No one paid the slightest attention to him.

When he made his report to Xerxes, the king did not realise the truth, namely that the Spartans were preparing to fight to the last. Far from it; to him their behaviour seemed quite ridiculous. He sent for Demaratos, a Spartan serving in the Persian army, and asked him about the details of the spy's information, hoping to find out what this strange behaviour meant. 'These men,' said Demaratos, 'are going to defend the pass. That's what they're preparing for. It's a rule among the Spartans that whenever they are about to risk their lives, they comb their hair carefully. But if you can beat these men and the remainder still at home in Sparta, then you can be quite sure that no other nation on earth will even try and resist you. These men you are facing are the bravest in Greece, and their kingdom the finest.'

Xerxes didn't believe him. For four days he waited for the Spartans to run away. On the fifth day, as they had still not made a move but, like the impertinent fools they were, obviously intended to stay put, Xerxes flew into a temper and sent the Medes and Kissians against them with orders to bring them back to him, alive. The Medes attacked, and were slaughtered in companies; others took their place and, in spite of tremendous losses, held their ground. It was clear to everyone, and not least to Xerxes himself, that his army was full of human beings but short of men.

After this disaster, the Medes were replaced by the King's Immortals, led by Hydarnes. They, at least, would have no trouble in putting an end to this nonsense. They moved into the attack. The result was precisely the same; in the

The Taÿgetos Mountains in Sparta. On these barren cliffs weak and unwanted babies were exposed and left to die.

narrow pass their greater numbers were useless, and their spears were shorter than the Greeks'.

The Spartans fought brilliantly, at the same time proving themselves to be experts against mere novices. They would turn their backs all together and pretend to be running for their lives. The Persians at once charged, screaming and banging, but just as the gap closed, the Spartans turned to face them and dealt untold havoc. True, the Spartans lost a few men, but the Persians, after trying regular and irregular troop formations, still got no nearer to capturing the pass and finally retreated.[4]

This incredible courage may, up to a point, have been inborn in the Spartans: they left any feeble-looking babies out on the Taygetos mountains to die. But those male children who remained were put through a gruelling course of training that started when they were

A Spartan shield, inscribed 'captured by the Athenians from the Spartans at Pylos' (see page 9).

seven. From that moment, fighting was the most important thing in a Spartan's life. Of course, the Spartans weren't unbeatable; but they thought they were, which was almost as good. It is interesting to see the reaction of the rest of the Greeks when at Pylos, nearly sixty years after the battle of Thermopylae described above, some Spartans actually surrendered:

Phalanxes in action. This diagram shows three phalanxes drawn up in battle-formation. When the two wings closed in round the enemy, there would be no escape. In the diagram the soldiers are holding their spears upright, not straight ahead as they are in the text.

Of all the events in the war between Sparta and Athens, this surrender of the Spartans was the thing which surprised the Greeks most. Everyone was sure that whether faced by starvation or any other threat the Spartans would never surrender their weapons, but would use them to fight to the death. There was some doubt whether the prisoners and the dead men were the same sort of soldiers. One of the Athenian allies actually asked one of the prisoners, as an insult, whether the real Spartans were the dead ones. The prisoner answered, 'It would be a smart arrow that could pick out a brave man from a coward' – the point of this retort being that in this case death had been a matter of luck.[5]

Even so, the Spartans went on to win the whole war, and occasional losses did not dim Sparta's legendary reputation:

Forward, sons of Sparta, holding your shields in front of you, wield your spears like men. Do not spare your lives: cowardice is not a Spartan virtue.

There the young man's spear is strong and the voice of the trumpet rises clearly, there in the broad streets lives Justice, the defender of good deeds.[6]

Close-packed infantry, armed with long spears, was the basic fighting force among the Greeks for 150 years after Marathon. When they were finally beaten by Philip of Macedon in 338, they were beaten at their own game. True, Philip did have cavalry, but he pinned his faith on the formation called the 'phalanx', which he had taken over from the Thebans and streamlined:

It is obvious, for all sorts of reasons, that as long as the phalanx keeps its proper shape and formation no force on earth can stand up to it when it is charging at full speed. In close battle formation, each man fully armed occupies 1 metre in breadth; the spears, originally planned to be 8 metres long, were later reduced

9

in practice to 7 metres: of this length, the hands are held 1 metre apart, and 1 metre is left behind the hands to balance the spear, so that when the soldier holds the spear in both hands in an attacking position, 5 metres of it is left sticking out in front of him. As long as the phalanx stays closely packed, which it ought to, from back to front as well as from side to side, the spears of ranks 2 to 5 will stick out ahead of the front rank by gradually descending amounts, down to those of the 5th rank, of which about 1 metre will be left showing. So each man in the front rank has five spears sticking out in front of him.

Those in the 6th rank and behind, as they are obviously not able to use their spears to attack with, do not all carry them held forward, but some carry them slanting over the shoulders of the men in front. This mass of spears protects the rear ranks from arrows or javelins which fly by mistake over the front ranks. At the same time, these men add weight to the attack of the front ranks, as well as making it quite impossible for them to run away.[7]

If you think about it, manoeuvring such a tightly packed body of men must have taken hours of practice. But, as the writer insists, the phalanx is useful *only* when it is under complete control. Philip's son, Alexander the Great, was not above using the phalanx to show off:

Alexander collected most of the infantry into a close body, 120 deep, with 200 cavalry on each side of them. He told them to keep quite silent, and to take his orders smartly. He then ordered the infantry to lift their spear-points, and next, at a word of command, to lower them as if for a charge. At a third word of command they swung the points now to the right, now to the left. He then moved smartly forward and took them through various movements on the wings. All this was done at high speed. Finally, he formed a wedge on the left side of the phalanx and led it into the attack.

But the natives had been so impressed by the efficiency and speed of these manoeuvres that they didn't stop to fight, but moved higher up the hill. At once, Alexander ordered the Macedonians to shout their war-cry and bang their shields with their spears. This was more than the natives could stand and they beat a hasty retreat to their town.[8]

On the outside of the phalanx were placed the two cavalry wings, one of which was always led by Alexander. The usual idea was to defeat the enemy on the wings and then, like the Greeks at Marathon, to swing in, catching the enemy between two fires. Alexander himself,

Fragment of the bronze rim of a shield. The rest of the shield was made of wood and layers of leather, and has perished.

Alexander the Great.

on his famous horse Bucephalus, was also able to move quickly to help any section of his army in trouble, and on occasion would even start the battle personally:

Meanwhile Darios' generals had assembled a large army to stop Alexander crossing the river Granikos. This crossing had to be made, as it was the gateway into Asia, but it had to be fought for; not only was the opposite bank guarded by Persians but it was bumpy and slippery, and the river itself was deep.

    Most of Alexander's lieutenants were frightened, some of them even bringing up the fact that it was May – because it had always been the custom for the Kings of Macedon to avoid fighting in May. Alexander countered this by saying, 'In that case we'll have April over again.' Then Parmenion, his second-in-command, thought the hour was perhaps rather late for taking risks. Alexander replied, 'I managed to cross the Hellespont. It would blush with shame if I

These Greek war-chariots are from the band at the top of a bronze mixing-bowl. The chariots are light and fast, and must have been very effective on a crowded battlefield.

allowed a mere river like this Granikos to scare me away', and charged into it with thirteen companies of cavalry.

Arrows hailed on them and the ground was treacherous, being littered with weapons and the bodies of horses, while the current continually pushed them off course and threatened to sweep the horses' legs from under them. Through it all, Alexander gave the impression of a madman, not giving orders sensibly but as if in some kind of fit.[9]

Sometimes these solo efforts misfired:

Alexander, now on top of the fortress wall, put his shield down and began to drive the Indians back inside, killing several of them with his sword, until at last he had cleared all defenders off that part of the wall. At last, as none of the enemy would come within fighting range, he stood there alone. His bodyguards were terrified that he would be killed and ran to the ladders, everyone trying to reach him first. But there were too many of them: the ladders broke under their weight and the men came crashing to the ground. The only way of helping Alexander had now disappeared.

Still none of the Indians dared to come within range of Alexander, but every archer in the place had his bow trained on him, including some from quite nearby in the town, brought closer still by the rising ground next to the wall. There could be no doubt on either side who it was standing there: the unbelievable bravery, like the flashing armour, told them it must be Alexander.

At this moment it occurred to him that if he stayed there on the wall he might easily be killed with nothing to show for it. If he jumped down into the fortress, there was a chance that he might cause a panic. Anyway, if he had to die, he would at least die fighting, in a way not likely to be forgotten.

No sooner said than done. He was now inside, with his back to the wall. The first Indian to attack him died on the point of his sword. Their leader was next to die, running at Alexander with more courage than skill. He drove off two more by hurling stones at them, then still more came within range, only to feel the edge of his sword. At last they learned their lesson: they kept out of range of the sword and stood in a semi-circle, pelting him with anything they could lay their hands on.

Three of the Macedonians, Peukestas, Abreas and Leonnatos, had managed to cling on to the wall when the ladders collapsed, and were now inside the fortress helping their commander. First, Abreas got an arrow in the face and was killed. Then Alexander himself was wounded. The arrow went through his tunic and sank into the upper part of his chest. An eye-witness tells us that one of his lungs was pierced and the wound bubbled with the escaping air. He was in terrible pain, but went on fighting. Suddenly, there was a rush of blood from the wound, such as you get from a pierced lung, and Alexander, almost unconscious, slumped forward over his shield.

Alexander's admiral, Nearchos, tells us that some of Alexander's friends blamed him for leading the attack so recklessly and taking risks which, for a general, were senseless. Alexander was angry with them for criticising him, all the more, I dare say, because he knew they were right. The answer is that he was fighting mad. Military glory was the one thing that mattered to him and, when there was a battle on, his own safety was the last thing he thought about. Plenty of men find there are pleasures they can't resist; in Alexander's case, it was fighting.[10]

These lone operations may remind us strongly of those described in Homer's *Iliad*. Alexander carried a copy of this poem in his luggage, and in many ways he managed to combine the dashing behaviour of Achilles with the more subtle military tactics of later times.

If anyone is surprised that Homer's heroes did not, like Alexander, ride on horseback, one look at a relief map of Greece should convince him that a quantity of cavalry would have been more trouble than it was worth in that mountainous country. In the Trojan war, horses were used only for pulling chariots, usually to get the heroes to the scene of the battle; after that, everything depended on them and their armour:

Then handsome Paris, husband of the lovely Helen, put the shining armour on his shoulders. First, he put round his legs a pair of sturdy greaves, fitted with silver clasps that fastened over the ankle. Next, he put on the breastplate which belonged to his brother Lykaon; even so, it fitted him. Over his shoulders he slung his sword, made of bronze and studded with silver, then a huge, thick shield, and on his mighty head he put a helmet, a fine piece of work crowned with a horsehair plume which nodded impressively. Finally, he took a strong spear which fitted into the palm of his hand. Menelaos similarly prepared himself for the coming battle.

So when they were both ready, they strode into the space between the two armies, such a terrifying sight that both Greeks and Trojans were dumb-founded. The two men stood quite close on the measured ground and angrily shook their weapons at each other.

First Paris let fly his spear, throwing a long shadow on the ground. It hit the round shield of Menelaos, but failed to pierce it. Then Menelaos in turn lifted his spear, with a prayer to Father Zeus, 'Zeus in Heaven, this Paris is the man who first wronged me. Let me be avenged on him, strike him down by my hands, so that future generations may shrink from rewarding a kind host with insults and injuries.'

With these words, he weighed the spear in his hand and flung it. It struck the round shield of Paris, through the gleaming shield it went and through the beautifully ornamented breastplate and ripped the tunic just under Paris' ribs. But he swerved aside and escaped a fatal injury. Menelaos now drew his sword, lifted it and brought it crashing down on the rim of Paris' helmet. But the sword fell from his hand in fragments. Raising his eyes to heaven, Menelaos groaned aloud, 'Father Zeus, you are the most deceitful of all gods. I swore I would have revenge on Paris for his insults, but now my sword has fallen to pieces in my hand and I have cast my spear without so much as grazing him.'

Then he grabbed hold of Paris' helmet, plume and all, and wrenching him round began to pull him towards the Greek lines. The tough strap of the helmet bit into Paris' tender throat, nearly strangling him, and Menelaos would certainly have dragged him off and won undying fame but for the quick

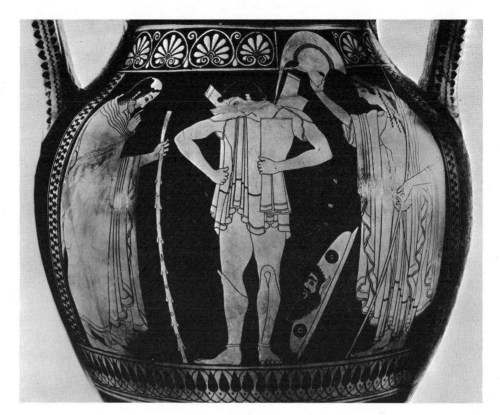

Hektor arming himself (from a vase-painting). He has already put on his greaves, and is pulling on his body-armour. On the right a servant holds his helmet, and his shield lies on the ground. The figure on the left seems to be offering advice.

thinking of Aphrodite, daughter of Zeus. She broke the strap, even though it was made of the toughest bull's hide, and the helmet came away in Menelaos' huge hand. With a mighty swing, he flung it into the ranks of the Greeks for his comrades to pick up. Then he advanced with his bronze spear, thirsting for the kill, but Aphrodite snatched Paris up in a moment, as immortals can, and hid him in a large cloud, before transporting him to the sweet-smelling comfort of his own bedroom.[11]

To us, such interruptions by gods and goddesses may at first seem unfair, but this was Homer's way of dealing with what we would call 'coincidences'. We are not really expected to believe that Paris vanished without a trace. It was just an unexpected thing for the strap to break at the very moment when Paris' life depended on it, and then he was so quick off the mark that by the time Menelaos turned round again he was gone, and was next seen by anyone hiding in his bedroom. Faced with Menelaos, no doubt most of us would have done the same.

The armour of the Homeric heroes was, as we see, very important to them; we are often given very detailed descriptions of, for example, the decorations on a shield. In later times, although commanders like Alexander were fond of dressing up, the armour and weapons in general do not seem to have been such personal possessions:

Some foreigner now gazes proudly at my shield. It wasn't the shield's fault: I abandoned it by a bush, and I didn't do it on purpose. But I did manage to escape with my life, so to hell with the shield! I can get another one just as good.[12]

Even though the writer was not being entirely serious, there is a point here: as armies got bigger, equipment had to be mass-produced and the soldier really could get another one just as good. But in the end, as at Marathon, it was always courage and training that counted. And when a battle was over, the Greeks seem often to have had in mind Achilles' treatment of the body of Hector:

Then Achilles dealt with Hector's body in a most shameful manner. On both his feet, he cut the tendons that run from the heel to the ankle and tied to them straps of ox-hide. These he fixed to his chariot, so that his enemy's head dragged on the ground. Then he threw Hector's magnificent armour into the chariot, jumped up himself and with a crack of the whip sent the horses galloping. The body of Hector was lost in a cloud of dust; his long, dark hair streamed out behind him and his head, given now by Zeus to Hector's enemies for them to dishonour in his own country, that noble head was black with the dirt of the plain.[13]

This was one of Achilles' actions which schoolboys were not meant to imitate. Alexander certainly, unless his enemies had been particularly troublesome, made a point of forgiving them; and after the Spartans had beaten the Persians at the battle of Plataia in 479, the Spartan general Pausanias made his feelings on the subject quite clear:

Among the Greek troops in this battle was a man from Aigina called Lampon,

Achilles fights Hektor. In this picture the heroes wear no body-armour, but rely on their shields and long spears. In the background two goddesses watch the contest.

an important citizen in his home town. After the battle he came rushing up to Pausanias with a most repulsive suggestion: 'Pausanias, this day you have done great deeds; heaven has granted you the privilege of saving Greece and allowed you to become the most famous man among all the Greeks. But there is still one thing you can do to increase your fame and to make sure that in future foreigners will think rather more carefully before they start interfering with us. When Leonidas was killed at Thermopylae, Mardonios and Xerxes had his head cut off and stuck on a pole. Now it is your turn, and you will make yourself popular not only in Sparta but in the whole of Greece. Stick Mardonios' head on a pole and avenge your uncle Leonidas.'

Lampon quite expected to be thanked for this suggestion. Pausanias replied: 'My dear sir, I must thank you for your kind words and for being so concerned about my future. You flatter me, my country and my success, but then you wipe it all out by suggesting that I mutilate a corpse, to increase my reputation. It is bad enough for Greeks to see savages doing such things without following their example. I sincerely hope I may never become a popular hero among the people of Aigina or anyone else who is amused by such behaviour. It is enough for me to be honoured in Sparta, and keep my hands free from sacrilege. As for Leonidas! Avenge him, you say? He has been avenged by those thousands of

17

This flat plain and scattered ruins are all that is left of Plataia today. The plain is fertile, well worth fighting over. The Persians chose such an open area because their huge army made them confident of overwhelming the enemy.

bodies out there, he and the Greeks who died with him at Thermopylae. And if you ever have such a suggestion to make again, keep well away from me. Now go, and think yourself lucky not to have been punished.' Lampon left without answering.[14]

Insulting a corpse has by now become an 'un-Greek' thing to do. It is an example of 'going too far', something the excitable race of Greeks always had to guard against. But they were as capable as anyone of seeing war as it really is:

This drawing, from a vase-painting, shows a Greek warrior and his wife in front of her loom. There are weights at the foot of each thread, and the finished cloth is wound upwards on rollers.

Hector's wife, Andromache, did not yet know what had happened. No messenger had come to tell her that her husband was outside the gates of Troy and she was still in her private apartment in the lofty palace, weaving a double length of purple cloth with an intricate pattern of flowers. She called out to the serving-maids to set up the large three-legged cauldron on the fire, so that Hector could have a hot bath when he came back from the battle. Poor girl, she was not to know that the bath would wait for ever, that grey-eyed Athene had already delivered him into the murderous hands of Achilles.

At this moment she heard a noise of howling and weeping from the city wall; her knees trembled and the shuttle fell from her hands to the floor. She spoke again to the maids: 'This way, two of you, follow me! That was the voice of Hector's mother. My heart is in my mouth, my knees are suddenly stiff. I know something terrible has happened to the family of Priam. I pray I may be wrong, but I am afraid the great Achilles has cut Hector off from the city and is now hunting him down on the plain, even now may have tamed the stubborn spirit which never let him skulk in the protection of the crowd. No, Hector was always out in front, the bravest of them all.'

So she rushed out of the palace like a madwoman, her heart beating wildly, and her maids ran behind her. She reached the crowd of men on the tower and stood on the wall, straining her eyes to see – her husband, at that instant being dragged in front of the city behind the swift, uncaring horses and away towards the ships of the Greeks. Then the plain went black before her eyes. Her senses left her and as she fell backwards the whole of her bright head-dress rolled to the ground, the metal frame, the headband, and the veil which Aphrodite had given her, on that day when Hector, in exchange for a handsome dowry, had come to take her from her father's house.[15]

EPITAPH ON THE SPARTANS AT THERMOPYLAE

Go, tell the Spartans, you who read this stone,
That we lie here, and that their will was done.[16]

2 · The enquiring mind

'For heaven's sake, stop asking questions! Why, why, why, all day long!' Perhaps we remember, as young children, being quelled by words such as these, and perhaps we also remember that desperate feeling – 'I must know NOW.' If so, we are already thinking like the ancient Greeks, many of whom went on questioning things until the day they died. This curiosity did not necessarily make them happy, or popular, but it prompted them to discover many things which lead in a direct line to the technological 'wonders' of the twentieth century.

But let us start at the beginning. It seems likely that at the time of Marathon (490 B.C.) only the middle and upper classes sent their children to school, but that in the course of the century the poorer

This drawing, from a vase-painting, shows two of the activities of a Greek school. One boy is learning to play the lyre, and another is learning to read. On the far right stands a father or interested bystander. Above the lyre-players' heads are a drinking-bowl and a brazier.

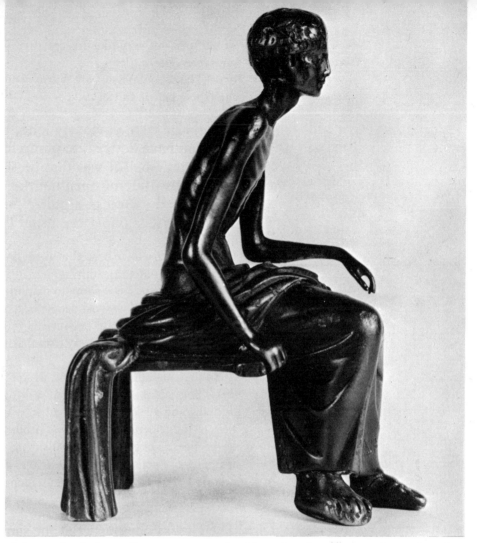

A young man – hungry for knowledge?

citizens in Athens began to get the idea that it was worth paying for. Pupils went through the first stage of schooling from the age of about six to fourteen, and richer or more ambitious ones might stay on for another four years or so. What was the point of this education? We have the following evidence from the prosecutor in a lawsuit:

The clerk of the court will now read out these laws for you, so that you can see that the lawmaker thought the well-educated child, when he grew up, would be useful to the city; but that when a child had a bad start to his education, he

21

would turn out very like this creature Timarchos here. Now let's hear these laws read out:

(1) The schoolmasters are not to open their schools before sunrise and are to shut them before sunset . . .[1]

The hours were obviously long, by our standards. But the idea was not, you have noticed, to pump facts into the pupil, to make sure he got a 'good job'; it was that he should be useful to the city.

But how did you turn out the useful citizen? This was a question that kept the Greeks arguing for years. Whatever the answer – if indeed there is one – the usual Greek curriculum was as follows:

Generally there have been four recognised subjects: writing, gymnastics, music and, some would add, painting; writing and painting as being practical and useful, gymnastics as leading to manliness. But as to music, there might well be some argument. Now most people practise it for pleasure. The educationists put it into the curriculum to begin with, following the needs of human nature which, as has been said many times, demands not only well-directed labour but enjoyable leisure as well.

So they introduced music not as something necessary – it is nothing of the sort – nor useful, in the way that writing is for business, housekeeping and studying and all sorts of practical activities, or as even painting is useful to help us judge better the works of professionals; and music doesn't make us fitter or stronger, like gymnastics. Music has nothing to do with any of these. So then it is a leisure activity, as many writers agree: in Homer's poem, Odysseus describes it as the best of all amusements when the company is in a good mood and 'the guests, sitting in their places, listen to a song'.[2]

The Greeks obviously felt the same way as we do about 'all work and no play', and music seems to have been just as important as the other subjects. The Spartans, in fact, did find a use for it; a military use, as we might have guessed. The two following descriptions make the point clear:

The Spartans now began to sing their war-songs, reminding each other of the glorious actions in which they had all shared. They knew that confidence born of experience is more reliable than any stirred up by fine words on the spur of the moment. Then the armies closed in. The Argives and their allies rushed

This vase-painting shows a lesson in lyre-playing. As well as another pupil and several bystanders, the artist has put in some unusual domestic pets.

forward in a violent fury, but the Spartans moved slowly to the measured music of a band of pipers. This is not done for any religious reason, but to make sure they keep in step while they're advancing and to stop the whole formation disintegrating, as so often happens when large armies move into the attack.[3]

When the formation was complete and the enemy within range, the Spartan king sacrificed a goat and gave orders for everyone to put on their garlands and told the pipers to play the tune of Kastor; at the same time the song of advance

23

began. The sight was a gripping and terrifying one as they marched to the rhythm of the music, keeping perfect order inside the phalanx and showing no sign of excitement, but moving calmly and confidently in time with the music towards the enemy. Surely, they felt no fear or passion, but had clear heads and hearts full of hope and courage, as though God was with them.[4]

A more detailed description of the inside of the classroom shows that some things haven't changed all that much, although the home discipline sounds rather strict:

Right from the time you are old enough to understand what they say to you, your nurse, your mother, your tutor and your father all try to make you as good as possible. Whatever you do or say, they are there to put you right by saying: 'This is right; that is wrong. This is a decent thing to do; that is shocking. This is polite; that is rude. Do this; don't do that.' As long as you do what you are told, there is no trouble. But if you don't they threaten you and beat you into shape, as if you were a twisted wooden plank.

When you are old enough to go to school, they make it clear to the masters that they are more interested in your being taught to behave properly than in your learning to read and write or to understand music. So when you have learnt your alphabet and can read, they put the very best books in front of you and make you learn them off by heart, stories with morals to them and ones which praise the deeds of the ancient heroes; the idea being to fire you with the enthusiasm to imitate them and try to behave like them. As well as all this, you are sent to a P.E. instructor to make your body as strong as your mind, so that you aren't let down in war or any other emergency by being physically feeble.

When you leave school, the state makes you learn the laws. These are intended as a guide for you to follow, to stop you wandering off the straight and narrow path. You remember how, when you were still rather shaky at writing, the master would mark in the letters on the slate lightly with a pencil, to help you in your own efforts? Well, that's also the way the laws are meant to work.[5]

Two things stand out as being different from a lot of modern education. Firstly, physical education was on a level with the other lessons and was thought of as being necessary for the scholar as well as for the soldier. Secondly, they did a lot of learning by heart.

P.E. was done in a gymnasium which, even without all the apparatus we have nowadays, was very much a place for the specialist.

Among the rooms which made up a gymnasium were the open-air wrestling place and a wet weather substitute, a room where the wrestlers were oiled, a room for ball games, a place to keep the dust which they sprinkled over the wrestlers when they had been oiled, dressing rooms, baths of hot, warm and cold water and, outside all these, porticoes with seats, where people could talk and study. Early in the nineteenth century A.D., archaeologists unearthed a gymnasium at Ephesus, on the south-west coast of what is now Turkey, and found it had been some 82 metres long and 64 metres broad. Whatever the height, it must have been an impressive building. One of the best examples of how seriously the Greeks felt about keeping fit is to be found in one of the Greek comedies, in a description of a particularly unathletic civil servant. One of the characters says:

Athens these days is crammed full of clerks and jumped-up monkeys always stirring up the workers. No one can even run in the torch race any more, they're all so unfit.

    Good God yes (comes the reply), I practically had a fit at the games the other day. Talk about laugh! There was this slowcoach, a great, fat, white slob, bent double he was, way behind everybody and making the most terrible fuss. He had to run the gauntlet through a bunch of locals; they gave him a real going-over, his belly, his ribs right round to his backside. What you might call slap-happy! Anyway, he blew out his torch and ran for it.[6]

'... *blew out his torch and ran for it'.*

The stadium, or race-track, at Delphi, seen from the judges' end. It is 185 metres long by 28 metres wide. The stone pillars on the right are nearly 3 metres high.

This is what the earlier writer meant about 'not being let down in an emergency by being physically feeble'.

As for the learning by heart, this was not just an easy way of keeping energetic Greek boys quiet, but was done 'to fire them with the enthusiasm to imitate the ancient heroes'. And they were made to learn more than the two or three short poems, which is all that most of us could quote. In this extract, two friends of Sokrates are talking:

This vase-painting shows a dithyrambos, *a man reciting Homer at one of the great Athenian festivals.*

KALLIAS So now, Nikeratos, will you tell us what knowledge you take most pride in?

NIKERATOS My father was determined to make a good man of me, so he made me learn the whole of Homer's poems, and even now I can repeat the *Iliad* and *Odyssey* off by heart.[7]

These two poems between them contain about 27,000 lines, something like 190,000 words. If Nikeratos had recited them both, at a fairly brisk speed, without coughs or pauses for water, it would have taken him about twenty hours. But without indulging in any such marathon, he had by him a guide for every action and a quotation to settle every argument. You may remember that the writer of the second extract on page 17 brought in some lines of Homer to clinch the matter.

When a poor boy left school at fourteen, he would probably follow his father's trade. But it would be wrong to say his education stopped there, as wrong as to say the girls of Athens weren't educated. As we have seen, the Greeks took a wide view of education; wider than we did in England until quite recently. For them, education wasn't just school, but was provided by talking, listening and going to the theatre, and these were things that everybody could do. They were far more at home with the spoken word than we are and placed tremendous importance on being able to persuade people, which is what is meant by 'rhetoric'. The Athenians enjoyed politics, and every citizen was entitled to express an opinion in the open-air Assembly. They also enjoyed bringing court-actions against each other, which gave them a chance to let off steam safely inside the framework of the law. So, although only rich men could afford to have their sons taught the art of rhetoric, several brilliant speakers were poor men who had taught themselves by listening to debates in the Assembly. Here is part of a speech by one of the most famous orators of ancient Greece, Demosthenes. His policy of resisting Philip of Macedon has ended in disaster. This is how he defends it:

As my opponent Aischines is determined to concentrate on these matters, I will answer his accusations and my answer, I fancy, will surprise him. Suppose

everyone had foreseen what was going to happen and you, Aischines, had prophesied it all with a great deal of shouting and bellowing, (though in fact you never opened your mouth) – even then it would have been the duty of Athens to do what she has done, that is if the fame of your ancestors or your future reputation means anything to you.

Of course, at the present moment it looks as if our policy has led to disaster, something which can happen to anybody if it's God's will. But at the time we adopted the policy, in our rôle as the leaders of Greece, if we had given in to Philip then, we would have borne the shame of betraying all our allies as well into his hands. There was no danger too great for our ancestors, when it came to defending the freedom of Greece; and if you, Aischines, had handed over this freedom without a struggle, who would not have spat on you? Not on Athens, nor on me, but on you. If we had left the other Greeks to carry on the fight against Philip, even though it was a failure – as, in fact, it has been – in God's name, how could we have looked visitors in the face when they came to Athens?

Never, in all our history, has anyone managed to persuade us to side with the strong against those who were in the right, or to lead a life of comfortable slavery; we have always fought to be the leaders of Greece and have taken risks in the pursuit of honour and glory. I know you yourselves regard this behaviour as right and proper, because out of all our ancestors it is the ones who followed these principles that you praise the most. And quite rightly. How can you help admiring a people who defied the Persians, left their town and country behind and took to the ships? And they chose as their general Themistokles, whose idea the evacuation was, and as for Kyrsilos, who thought they really should do what they were told by the Persians, they stoned him and their wives stoned his wife. Athenians who had fought at Marathon did not intend to listen to anyone, politician or general, who was going to turn them into docile slaves. No, they would rather have died, if they could not be free.

So if you, now, go on record as saying that I gave you bad advice, then you will appear not as victims of bad luck, but as men who made a mistake. But it was not, gentlemen, it was not a mistake to fight for the freedom and safety of the whole of Greece. Think of our ancestors who led the Greek army at Marathon, think of those who fought at Plataia and manned the ships at Salamis and Artemision, and all those brave, honest men who now lie in the public cemetery. The state thought they ought all to be given an honourable burial – note this, Aischines – not just those who were successful or those who won. And the state was right. They all acted like true men and took what Fate had in store for them. Very well then, you filthy little bookworm . . .[8]

This coin shows Philip of Macedon. His gold coins were so well made and so wide-spread, that the word 'Philips' came to mean 'coins' (just as 'Louis d'or' did much later in France).

Right: *The Heroes' Cemetery in Athens, as it is today. In the background stands the Akropolis, with the Parthenon roof just visible.*

Opposite: *Demosthenes. This statue was carved about fifty years after his death. The artist may have tried more to show a wise, dignified old man rather than give an accurate likeness of Demosthenes.*

Throughout the speech, he carefully *doesn't* mention that all the ancient battles were Greek victories. He just wants to make his audience feel that they have been as brave as the Greeks at Marathon; he does not want to remind them of the very different results of the two battles. Of course, we shall never know what Demosthenes in full cry sounded like – how did his tone of voice change when he got to 'filthy little bookworm'? – but we do know something of his training:

They say that once, when he had been hissed off the platform, he was on his way back home with his head wrapped up in his cloak, feeling very depressed, and he met a friend of his, an actor called Satyros. As they walked along, Demosthenes began to grumble and complain that he worked harder at his speeches than any of the other speakers in Athens and that he had worn himself out doing so, but still he couldn't get across to the mob; they ignored him and listened instead to drunkards, common seamen and uneducated louts. 'Yes,' said Satyros, 'but I'll soon fix that for you. Can you recite some Euripides off by heart, or some Sophokles?'

Demosthenes duly recited and then Satyros repeated the same passage after him. The whole thing suddenly took on a new shape: movements, expressions, gestures, all were fitted perfectly to the words, in fact to Demosthenes the passage sounded like something quite different. This convinced him how much the effect of a speech depends on its delivery; if you ignore this side of it, it's a waste of time inventing strings of marvellous words.

He then went and built himself an underground practice-room, and he would be there all day, every day, working on his gestures and the tone of his voice. Often, he was there for two or three months at a time and shaved the hair off one side of his head so that, even if anyone came wanting to see him, he would be too embarrassed to come out.

And we have more evidence of how hard he worked from Demetrios, who says he got this from Demosthenes himself when he was an old man. His speech wasn't at all clear and he lisped, so he forced his tongue to work properly by putting pebbles in his mouth and making speeches through them. He would also work on his voice while he was running along or climbing a steep hill, and would puff his way through speeches and reams of poetry.[9]

From the same author comes a story which shows persuasion at work, and the value of learning by heart. The story depends really on three things. (1) Those involved had to know the legend of Elektra, the daughter of King Agamemnon, and how, according to Euripides, she was thrown out of the palace after her father's murder and forced to live the life of a peasant, exiled and in disgrace; (2) the speaker had to have learnt part of that play by heart; (3) he had to see how one particular bit of the play could be used to persuade.

The scene is the camp of the Spartans, who are besieging Athens at the end of their long war:

So Lysander, the Spartan general, received the surrender of the whole Athenian navy, apart from twelve ships, and with it the walls of Athens. The date was 20 September 404, the seventy-sixth anniversary of the defeat of the Persians at Salamis.

Lysander lost no time in making plans to change the government of the city. The Athenians resented this and said so in no uncertain terms, but he sent them back a message, accusing them of breaking their word. By now, the walls should have been pulled down, but there they still were; the whole future of Athens would have to be considered again, as they couldn't be trusted to keep their promises.

According to some reports, there was even talk among the Spartan allies of turning the whole population into slaves, and a Theban called Erianthos suggested the city should be destroyed and made into grazing land. But then, when all the allied generals and their staff were at an official banquet, at the symposion one of the delegates from Phokis began to sing the opening chorus of Euripides' *Elektra*, which begins:

CHORUS Elektra, daughter of Agamemnon, I have come to your country hovel . . . with news from one of the local mountain farmers. In two days time the people of Argos will be celebrating a festival and all the young girls will be dancing in honour of the goddess Here.

ELEKTRA My friends, there is no joy for me in putting on finery and gold necklaces, and I shall not be there to lead the young girls in the stamp and whirl of the dance. My nights and days are spent in misery and tears.

Then they were all ashamed and disgusted with themselves for thinking of destroying a city which was so famous and which had produced such men as Euripides.[10]

Not only that but, of course, the figure of Elektra, once a princess in a palace, now a poor farmer's wife in a hovel, reminded them – as it was meant to – of the glorious past of the now humbled Athens. In the original Greek, the storyteller quotes only as far as the first phrase. He felt sure his readers would know how it went on.

The word 'rhetoric' may sound rather pompous to us, but not all Greek rhetoric by any means was as serious as our example from Demosthenes. The orator's training, as well as giving him the power to make fighting speeches like that one, also gave him a command of wit and sarcasm which was meant to deflate rather than persuade. The man who saved the Greeks at Salamis, Themistokles, was not above using these weapons to silence his critics:

And when, in the middle of the conference, a man from Eretria began to say something he didn't agree with, Themistokles turned on him. 'So you've got to have an opinion on the war too, have you? You're like the cuttlefish, all beak and no belly.'[11]

And again, after the Greek victory at Salamis:

Themistokles.

Below: Ostrakon *(voting-tablet) from the Athenian assembly, c. 480 B.C. The writing means 'Themistokles – OUT!'*

A man from the little island of Seriphos said to Themistokles that he was famous not thanks to his own efforts, but just because he happened to be an Athenian. 'You've got something there,' said Themistokles; 'I wouldn't be famous if I came from Seriphos – nor would you if you came from Athens.'[12]

Both these remarks are very Greek, in their neatness and in their complete unanswerability. But again, wit and sarcasm are not the whole picture. A study of rhetoric was useful, certainly, but there was little point in being witty if you were a bad man; Themistokles, for all his quick repartee, was no angel and ended his life in exile. And so we get back to the question of how to produce the good all-rounder. The child's parents could help, and, later, so could his wife:

We parents put up with the misbehaviour of our friends; why not that of our sons? We often say nothing when our slaves get drunk and have hangovers. If you've been stingy in the past, try and be a bit more generous; if you've been hard on him, be more forgiving. He has tricked you, perhaps, with the help of a slave; control you anger. He has stolen two of your cattle from the farm, or he came in yesterday in a cloud of alcohol; forgive him. Or stinking of perfume; hold your tongue.

This is the way to cure the juvenile delinquent. But those who are particularly wild, and refuse to take any notice of you, should be married off. That's the surest way to make them toe the line.[13]

But this could hardly be called an academic training in goodness, so it is not surprising that some Greek should begin thinking hard about the problem, and ask not so much 'why?', which to them was obvious, as 'what?'

The most famous of the Greeks to apply his mind to this problem was Sokrates, who lived in Athens through the period of the war against Sparta. Two of the basic questions he asked were: (1) What is the goal that human beings should aim at? (2) How are they to get there? In fact, he never succeeded in answering even the first question to his own satisfaction, but he had fun trying. His method was to argue with anybody who fancied his own opinions and strike sparks off them. The next three extracts all come from an argument he had with a wealthy young man called Meno, who thought he knew all the answers:

MENO Do you mean this seriously, Sokrates, that you don't know what virtue is? Can I go home and quote you on that?

SOKRATES And you can also say that, as far as I know, I've never met anyone else who did either. Now what about you? What do you think it is?

M Oh, that's easy. If it's virtue in a man that you're talking about, then anyone can see what that is: being efficient in public affairs, helping his friends, doing down his enemies and keeping out of trouble himself. Or virtue in a woman: that's being a good housewife, keeping a careful eye on the food expenses and doing what her husband tells her. Then there are the virtues for girls and boys and old men, citizens or slaves; and lots more. I don't see how anyone can say he doesn't know what virtue is.

S This must be my lucky day. I just wanted one virtue and here you are offering me a whole swarm. Seriously though, talking of swarms, suppose I ask you: 'What is a bee? What makes up the "beeness" of a bee?' and you said there were lots of kinds of bee, I would then say: 'There may be lots of kinds, but are they different in "beeness"? Or are they perhaps different in something else like size or beauty?' Now what do you say to that?

M I say that as far as 'beeness' goes, they are all the same.

S Fair enough. And if I then said: 'Now this is what I'm really after. What is this quality they all have in common?' Could you answer that one?

M Yes.

S All right then. Treat the virtues in the same way. There may be lots of different ones, but they must all have something in common which makes them virtues. Take health, or size or strength. For example, is health the same thing for everybody, and in animals too?

M Yes.

S What about size and strength? If a woman is strong, is it the same thing making her strong as in a man? I would say that strength is strength wherever it is, in a man or a woman, but perhaps you disagree?

M No, I agree.

S And will virtue then be different, whether it occurs in a child or an old man, or a man or a woman?

M I don't really feel virtue is the same sort of case as the others.[14]

'I don't really feel . . .' The bumptious young man isn't quite as happy as he was. A bit later, he tries to define 'virtue' in a different way:

s So you define virtue as the desire for good things and the ability to get them. It's quite possible you're right. The ability to get hold of good things, you say?

m That's right.

s What do you mean by 'good things'? Do you mean health and money?

m Yes, money and important positions in the state.

s Is that all?

m Well, everything like that.

s I see, So then, 'Meno's Law' states that to get hold of gold and silver is virtue. Does one have to get hold of it legally, or doesn't that matter?

m Of course it does.

s So another bit of virtue must also be involved, justice or moderation or decency; without them, although your definition might lead to virtue, it can't really *be* virtue.

m No, you obviously can't have virtue without justice and the rest.

s Then to possess gold and silver one doesn't have to be virtuous, any more than one does to be poor. The real answer is that any action which depends on justice is virtuous, and any one that doesn't is not.

m There seems no way round it; you must be right.[15]

Round Two to Sokrates. We are hardly surprised when, a minute later, the poor young man is saying:

m Sokrates, before I came to you people warned me; 'He's unsure of everything himself, and makes everybody else the same.' Right now I feel like the victim of some piece of witchcraft, as though you'd paralysed me with some spell or other. If you'll forgive me, I think that to look at, and in other ways as well, you are just like the sting-ray that infests the sea, the sort that numbs you whenever you touch it. My brain and my mouth are both paralysed and I can't think of anything to say. If you ask me, you'd better not leave Athens and live elsewhere; abroad, as a foreigner and going on the way you do, you'd soon find yourself in prison as a sorcerer.[16]

Meno at least had the good sense to climb down then and admit he didn't know either what virtue was. But some of Sokrates' more 'im-

Sokrates. On one occasion, during a performance of The Clouds *(see page 86), he is said to have held a pose like this in the theatre, in a daydream, for over three hours.*

Aristotle. This is a much later Roman statue. It is probably not so much a likeness of Aristotle himself, as a Roman artist's idea of what a great thinker looked like.

portant' opponents, some of whom earned their living by teaching virtue, couldn't afford to give in so easily. Tempers were lost and Sokrates became unpopular with the wrong people. In the end, he was executed by order of the state for 'corrupting the young men'.

Philosophers like Sokrates were also interested in what we lump together as 'science'. Aristotle, the tutor of Alexander the Great, wrote on (in alphabetical order) agriculture, anatomy, anthropology, astronomy, biology, botany, mathematics, mechanics, meteorology, physics, physiology and psychology, and made very important contributions to most of them. Here is a passage of his on the fish's sense of smell:

Generally speaking, if the bait is not fresh, the fish won't touch it. Also, you have to vary the bait according to the species, and they distinguish these baits by using their sense of smell. For example, some kinds of fish live in caves and to catch them the fishermen daub the mouth of the cave with pickles, which have a strong smell, and this method soon works. Some people also claim that they can always tell when their own blood has been spilt in the water, and leave the area at high speed.[17]

In this extract and in the three passages of Sokrates' conversation, we can see the same desire to get to the bottom of things: fact is more important than feeling. Meno may think he knows what virtue is, but facts prove otherwise. Because fish don't seem to sniff, we might think they can't smell, but again facts prove otherwise.

The process was the same in Greek medicine. One of the most famous Greek doctors was Hippokrates; these were his methods:

We doctors base our judgments on what we know of disease generally, and of each disease in particular; on what we know of the illness we are treating, of the patient, of his treatment so far and his previous doctor. We take into account the prevailing climate, where the patient comes from, his way of life, his job, his age, his conversation, mannerisms, silences, thoughts, whether he is a good sleeper or not, his dreams – what sort they are and how often he has them – any picking or scratching, hysteria, discharges, sneezing or vomiting. We follow most carefully the way in which the illness progresses to its most acute phase, checking details like sweating, coldness, stiffness, coughing, sneezing,

The ruins of the temple of healing at Kos, birthplace of Hippokrates. The pillars on the second level give an idea of the size of the shrine: they are over 6 metres high.

hiccuping, heavy breathing and internal bleeding. It is our job to pay attention to all these things and see what they lead to.[18]

Finally, let us look at two examples from Greek mathematicians:

Achilles runs ten times as fast as a tortoise. But if the tortoise is given, let us say, 1000 metres start it can't be overtaken. Because when Achilles has covered the 1000 metres, the tortoise is still 100 metres in front of him; when he has covered these 100 metres, the tortoise is 10 metres in front of him; when he has covered these 10 metres . . .[19]

37

So, can Achilles ever win? This is one of the 'paradoxes' of a philosopher called Zeno, who was born about the time of Marathon. Thales, the subject of the final extract, was born over 100 years before that and left no written works. He was obviously a better mathematician than the man who wrote (some 600 years later) the following account of his demonstration.

The King of Egypt regarded Thales as an extraordinary person for several reasons, but he was particularly impressed by his achievement in measuring a pyramid's height without making any calculations or using any instruments. Thales simply stuck his walking-stick into the sand at the tip of the pyramid's shadow; this, with the rays of the sun, made two triangles (see diagram) and he pointed out that the proportion between the two shadows was the same as that between the pyramid and the walking-stick.[20]

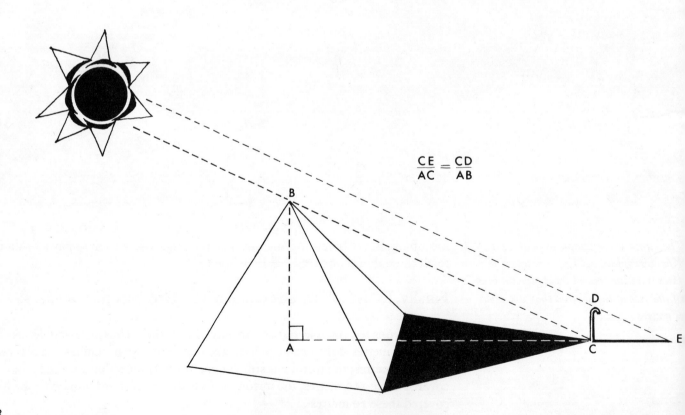

$$\frac{CE}{AC} = \frac{CD}{AB}$$

3 · Ships and the sea

As soon as rosy-fingered Dawn had touched the sky, Odysseus put his cloak and tunic on. The nymph dressed herself in a light, graceful garment that shone like silver, and fastened a golden belt round her waist, and a veil about her head. Then she turned her attention to great-hearted Odysseus' departure. She gave him a polished adze, and a great two-headed axe of bronze, with a tight-fitting handle of polished olive-wood, fitted to his grip. Then she led him to a distant part of the island, where tall trees grew, poplars, alders and pines whose heads touch heaven. The wood was old and dry, long since sapless: it would float easily and well.

When she had shown him the wood, Kalypso left, and Odysseus set to work at once. He felled twenty trees, rough-trimmed them with the axe, and then smoothed them down till they were straight and true. Then Kalypso brought him drills, and he bored holes in the timbers and fitted them together, fastening them with clamps and wooden pegs. He made a keel as wide as a broad-bottomed merchant-ship, built by a master-carpenter, and fitted platforms to it at bows and stern, fastened to stout ribs. The whole job was finished off with planking down the sides, and a superstructure of woven wickerwork to protect him from the sea.

Next he placed in position the mast and its yard-arm, and a steering-oar to control the boat. On the bottom he piled logs for ballast. Then, with cloth supplied by Kalypso, he made a sail, and lashed it skilfully in position with the usual braces, sheets and halyards. When everything was finished and the boat was ready, he dragged it down on rollers into the calm sea.[1]

This clever piece of ship-building took Odysseus only four days; on the fifth the goddess provisioned the boat with the same superhuman simplicity:

Kalypso gave Odysseus fine clothes to wear, and placed two flasks in the boat, one of dark wine and the other, larger one of water. In addition there was a leather bag of corn, and a selection of delicious cooked meats.[2]

Odysseus sailed for eighteen days on this diet, until his boat was swamped in a storm, and he was washed up on the shore of Phaiakia, ready for the next instalment of his adventures.

More ordinary men found life a little more difficult. When Odysseus' boat was finished he launched her in half a sentence, 'dragging her down on rollers into the calm sea'. No fuss, no bother. But when Jason and his crew launched *their* ship *Argo*, to go and find the Golden Fleece, the whole process was much more awkward:

First they piled their clothes on a dry, flat rock washed clean and smooth by winter storms long ago. Then, guided by Argos, they set to work. They fastened ropes tightly round the hull, pulling them taut on each side, so that the planks would cling to the bolts, whatever the force of the opposing water. Next they dug a trench the width of the ship right down from the bows into the sea. The further they went, the deeper they dug, placing polished rollers at the bottom of the trench, and easing *Argo* down on them so that she would glide smoothly and easily into the water.

Up above, protruding about 50 cm on either side, they fastened oars to the thole-pins. Then the whole crew took up their positions, hands and chests on the oars, ready to heave as soon as the word was given. Tiphys leaped on board to shout orders and make sure they all pushed at the same moment. He gave a loud cry, and they heaved forward with all their strength, and started *Argo* moving. Then, edging forward and shouting encouragement to each other, they forced her on. *Argo* began moving, faster and faster; the rollers creaked and groaned as they took the weight, and black smoke rose up as the timbers chafed together.

At last *Argo* reached the sea, and they hauled her inshore and moored her. Then they fitted the oars back round the thole-pins, put up the mast, and loaded the well-made sails and all the provisions for the voyage.[3]

Of course, *Argo* was very much bigger than Odysseus' boat – there were over fifty men in the crew. This may seem small, by our standards, for an ocean-going vessel. But it was in ships like this that the Greeks built up their formidable reputation as sea-farers. The ships were powered by oars or a single sail, and steered by a long broad-

Opposite: *Dionysos, god of wine, sailing in a simple boat, not much different from the one built by Odysseus.*

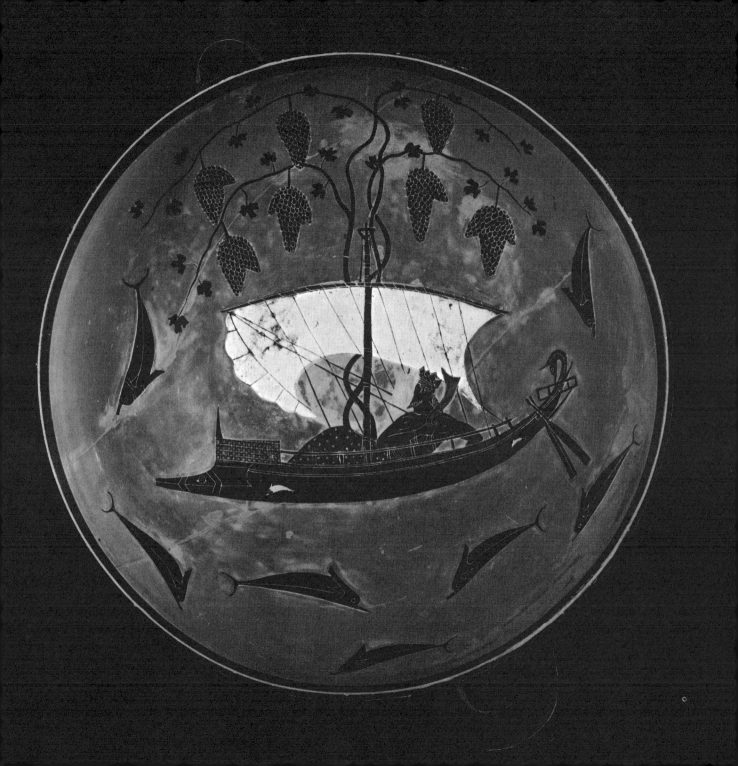

A ship about the size of the Argo, *cruising in calm waters. You can see the steering oars at the back, and the wide single sail.*

bladed oar manipulated by a single helmsman. There was no way of navigating except by the sun and stars, so that sailing out of sight of land was a risky business. Clearly the crews must have been highly-trained, experienced men:

When they came down to the ship and the sea, they stowed all the food and drink away in the hold, and spread a sheet and blanket for their passenger on the stern platform where he could sleep in peace. He went quietly on board and lay down. The crew, who knew their job well, took their places on the rowing-benches, and unfastened the mooring-rope from its pierced stone. Then, putting their backs into the work, they began to churn the sea to foam with their oars. Just as a team of four stallions, responsive to the whip, gallops eagerly across the plain, heads tossing and feet flying; just so did the ship rear proudly from the dark water that ran and bubbled away astern. On she sped, so light and fast that not even a wheeling hawk, the fastest thing that flies, could have kept pace with her.[4]

But even so their skill and daring must often have seemed useless because their boats were so primitive and fragile. Here is an account of how *Argo* escaped the Clashing Rocks – possibly icebergs – at the mouth of the Bosphorus:

When they reached the narrow, winding straits, walled in by cliffs, they felt the current swirling against them, and were filled with a great fear. Their ears rang with the grinding and crashing of the Rocks, and the endless roar of water against the cliffs.

Then Euphemos took a dove, as the gods had instructed, and went up on the ship's bows. Tiphys gave the rhythm to the rest of the crew, and they rowed eagerly on, hoping that by using all their strength they could drive *Argo* safely through the channel. They rounded a bend and saw the Rocks opening – the last men on earth to see that sight. Their hearts sank; but Euphemos let the dove go, and as they all raised their heads to look, it flew straight for the gap between the Rocks.

Suddenly the Rocks rushed at one another, and met with a thunderous crash. A storm of foam and white spray leaped up, and the sea groaned and thundered till the sky echoed. Water roared into the hollow caverns at the foot of the cliffs, and a cloud of spray rose high above them. *Argo* was snatched by the current and whirled round in a helpless circle.

But although the Rocks had snapped shut on the dove's tail-feathers and torn them off, she herself had got through unharmed. When they saw this the crewmen gave a great cheer, and Tiphys shouted to them to row as hard as they could, as the Rocks were opening again. They obeyed him, trembling.

Then the current took hold of them, and whirled them round towards the Rocks. Panic seized them; death hovered overhead. They were so far in that they could see the channel opening out on either side, when all at once a huge wave billowed up in front of them, curved like an overhanging rock. They cowered in fear, sure that it would fall on them and crush them. But Tiphys eased the ship round at the last moment, and the wave slipped harmlessly under her keel, lifting her high in the air and washing her right past the Rocks.

Euphemos ran down among his companions, shouting to them to row as hard as they could. Eagerly they obeyed him, but the current was still too strong; their oars bent like bows, and they were swept back three metres for every two they travelled.

Then another huge wave rushed down on them, and *Argo* rolled end-on and plunged through the roaring water. She was washed back between the Clashing Rocks, and wedged there unable to move. The current ebbed and flowed, and the Rocks rumbled and roared on either side; but *Argo* was stuck fast.

That was when Athene came down and took a hand. She thrust the solid rock aside, freed *Argo* and sent her speeding through the channel. On the ship flew, winged like an arrow; but even so, as the Rocks crashed shut, they snapped off the very tip of the superstructure at the stern. Apart from that, they were safely through, and Athene soared back up to Heaven, her task complete.[5]

The Mediterranean and Aegean Seas are still notorious for the suddenness and violence of their storms; many twentieth-century sailors have stories of bad weather just as graphic as this one by Aischylos:

Fire and water, those old enemies,
Made common cause, and came to kill us.
In the night disastrous waves arose
From Thrace that took our ships and drove them
Hard into each other's flanks. Overhead
A mad shepherd savaged his flock
With rain and hail; ship butted ship
Like leaping rams at play; the sky screamed.
Next morning the whole sea had flowered
With wrecks and bits of men.[6]

With storms like these to face, it may seem surprising that anyone ever put to sea at all. But quite apart from those who actually *enjoyed* it, large numbers of Greeks had no choice but to travel. Some even put the hazards of sea-voyaging to most ingenious uses. The normal way of trading was this: you bought a ship, and borrowed money to buy a cargo. You exported this cargo, sold it for a profit, and bought a new cargo to bring home. When this too was sold – again for a profit – you repaid the original loan. So everyone was happy: the banker made 12% interest on his month's investment (and sometimes very much more); and the shipowner made a handsome profit on the sale of his cargoes.

So far this is legitimate trading, but what happens if the ship sinks at sea? The rule in Athens was that if this happened, the loan was immediately cancelled, and the shipowner could also claim his insurance money. Hence some very ingenious frauds, like the one following,

In this vase-painting, king Arkesilas and his servants are weighing a valuable cargo of silphium *(a herb) ready for export.*

attempted by two unsuccessful crooks called Zenothemis and Hegestratos.

Hegestratos was the owner, and Zenothemis was in his pay. They each borrowed money in Syracuse. Hegestratos agreed that if enquiries were made, he would tell Zenothemis' creditors that there was a great deal of corn in the ship belonging to Zenothemis, and Zenothemis promised to tell Hegestratos' creditors that the ship's cargo was Hegestratos' own property. Since one of them owned the ship, and the other was a passenger on board, everyone believed what they said about one another.

When they got the money they sent it home to Marseilles; no cargo was loaded on the ship at all. The arrangement with the bankers was the usual one: the loan would only be repaid if the ship reached its destination safely. But

Zenothemis and Hegestratos planned to scuttle the ship, and so cheat their creditors.

So one night, when they were two or three days' journey from land, on their way to Athens, Hegestratos went down into the hold and began cutting a hole in the bottom. Up on deck Zenothemis carried on as though nothing was happening. But a sudden noise warned everyone that something was going on in the hold, and they rushed down to find out what it was. Hegestratos was caught red-handed, and when he saw he was cornered, he jumped overboard to escape arrest. He meant to land in the dinghy; but missed because of the darkness, and was drowned. So he came to a richly-deserved bad end – the same, in fact, as he'd planned for everyone else.

His accomplice Zenothemis, left on board ship, at first exclaimed at the wickedness of the crime, as though he'd just heard about it. Then he tried to persuade the helmsman and the rest of the crew to take to the boats and leave the ship at once, as it was sinking fast with no hope of being saved. He hoped that in this way what they planned would happen: the ship would sink and the bankers be defrauded. But he failed in this, because the banker's agent on board promised the crew a large reward if they saved the ship.

Through the efforts and bravery of the crew, and the help of the gods, the ship eventually reached Kephallenia. Zenothemis now pretended that it wasn't on its way to Athens at all, but had just come from there, and that he and the cargo were making for Marseilles, the home port of owner, captain and bankers alike. But this didn't work either, as the authorities at Kephallenia knew very well that the ship was not only registered in Athens, but was on its way there on this occasion.

These crimes and lies would have been enough for any ordinary man; but Zenothemis wasn't finished yet. When the ship finally reached Athens, he had the nerve to claim that the non-existent corn was his own property, and had been all the time. He even took the bankers to court to prove it.[7]

Zenothemis, we may presume, lost his case. He and Hegestratos traded in Marseilles, stopping in Sicily *en route*. Other Greek traders travelled further afield: through the Bosphorus into the Black Sea, up the Danube, down the Nile, and even into such remote areas as the Persian Gulf, the Red Sea and (via the Straits of Gibraltar) the Atlantic. Herodotos even describes a voyage made all the way round Africa:

Model of a merchant-ship. You can see from the model why these small, squat ships hugged the coast whenever they could.

A Phoenician warship. Notice the sleek lines, built for speed, and the ram at the front, for holing your enemy below the water-line.

We know that Africa is surrounded by water on every side, except where it joins on to Asia. The first person to prove this, so far as I know, was king Nekos of Egypt. He began a canal from the Nile to the Arabian Gulf, and then sent some Phoenician sailors to try and sail round the whole continent, through the Pillars of Herakles, and so back to Egypt.

The Phoenicians set out, and sailed from the Red Sea into the Southern Ocean. Each year when autumn came they landed and sowed corn, in whatever part of Africa they happened to be. They waited until it was ripe, then harvested it and sailed on again. In this way they were well into their third year before they reached the Pillars of Herakles and so came back to Egypt. They said – and it seems a ridiculous story to me – that throughout their voyage round Africa the sun stayed always on their right-hand side.[8]

Remember that this voyage was probably made in a boat no bigger than the *Argo*. The detail about the sun, at the end, confirms the authenticity of the story (the Cape of Good Hope is in the Southern Hemisphere).

The sailors who sailed round Africa were Phoenicians. The Greeks

Athenian grain-ship (left) and war-galley (right). This vase-painting probably shows pirates in action.

themselves usually avoided exceptional trips like this, and concentrated on short voyages in their own area. Crete and Sicily to the south, and the Bosphorus to the north, would be regarded as the limits of 'normal' travel. Crete, in fact, had once been the centre of a great sea-empire, and was in its time as powerful as Athens in the Classical period. And, like the Cretans, the Athenians made themselves the leaders of Greece very largely by means of their supremacy at sea.

The following extract from Thukydides shows Athenian glory and power at its height. It is a description of the great war-expedition that set out for Sicily in 415 B.C. – a glittering, magnificent fleet the Athenians must have thought invincible.

49

No expedition so costly or magnificent had ever before sailed from a single city. They were prepared for a long absence, and ready to fight either on land or by sea, whichever was required. Both the State and the individual shipowners had spent lavishly: the public treasury provided each sailor with a drachma a day, and supplied 100 empty ships, 60 to be fitted out as fast fighting-vessels and 40 as troop-carriers. The shipowners manned these vessels with the best crews available, supplementing the wages paid by the State to rowers and petty-officers, and providing figure-heads and other equipment of the most expensive type. Each owner was anxious that his ship should be the fastest and best equipped in the whole fleet.

The soldiers were hand-picked men, too, from the top of each list. There was great rivalry between them over arms and personal equipment. Everyone was determined to be the best-armed and best-disciplined man in Athens. The rest of Greece marvelled, thinking the whole thing more like a ceremonial parade than an expedition against real enemies. Certainly no greater or more glittering force had ever set out, or with higher hopes of victory.

When all the equipment was loaded, and the crews were in position, a trumpet blew for silence, and the usual prayers were offered up. A single herald led them, and his words were repeated by all the crews together. Wine was poured into the mixing-bowls, and on each ship officers and crew made libations from gold and silver cups. Everyone on the shore joined in these prayers and offerings, both the actual citizens and any other sympathetic bystanders.

At the end of the ceremony a hymn was sung, and the fleet set sail. They went ahead in line for some way, then broke ranks and raced each other as far as Aigina. From there they made their way to Kerkyra, where the other allied forces were waiting.[9]

How proud and self-confident they were, beginning a war-expedition with a race! Certainly up to now the sea-gods had favoured Athens. It was under her leadership that the combined Greek fleet had routed the vast Persian invasion at Salamis in 480 B.C. This had been one of the proudest moments in Greek history, and certainly some of the Athenian sailors, as they put out past Aigina into the open sea, must have remembered Aischylos' magnificent account of that earlier battle. It was written some years after Salamis, in the form of a speech made to the Persian royal court by a messenger from the battle-front; but even in the words of a defeated enemy, Aischylos' intention was to

The Straits of Salamis today. It is hard to imagine a sea-battle taking place in such a quiet, calm stretch of water.

glorify the naval skill of the Greeks, and the strategy of the Athenian commander Themistokles.

As the drawing on page 52 shows, the huge Persian fleet had the Greeks hemmed in between the island and the mainland, and were only waiting for their chance to close in and destroy them. But the Greeks were not finished yet. They decided to keep the enemy up all night, and so tire them out before the battle started. This extract shows the cunning way this was done, and the triumphal result:

A soldier – Athenian – came to Xerxes and said: 'My lord, the Greeks are afraid. They'll wait for dark, then leap on board and row for their lives.' Xerxes believed this – the gods saw to that. He sent word round his captains to lie low till the sun set. Then, under cover of dark, they were to divide the fleet in three: one group to row round the island, the others to stop up the exits to the open sea. 'If any Greeks escape,' he said, 'you'll pay with your heads.'

He was totally confident; but the gods had other plans. Obediently, well-disciplined, our men fastened their oars ready, then went back on shore and had dinner. As soon as it was dark, the rowers and the fighting-men embarked and went to their places. Calling out to each other, they rowed out in formation across the straits. The captains kept them rowing to and fro all night.

But the Greeks didn't move. All night they waited, till the dawn appeared on her milk-white horses. *Then* they cheered – cheered till the rocks echoed.

Salamis: before the battle. This artist's impression shows how easily the narrow straits could be turned into a bottleneck, and the advantage light, fast ships would have over heavier ones.

These weren't cowards, running; these were fighting-men gathered for the kill. Our hearts went cold with fear. We heard a trumpet blaze, and the steady thud of oars. Out they came, the right wing first, then the rest in good order. And all the time we heard their battle-cry: 'On, sons of Greece! Set free your country, your children, wives, homes of your ancestors and temples of your gods! All depend on you now: fight!'

On our side we raised our Persian war-cry, and the fight began. Ship battered into ship; bronze beaks tore at the woodwork, stripping it from the keels. We held them at first; but gradually they hemmed us in till our ships tangled and there was no way out, no way to help a friend. Oars smashed, sterns caved in. And still the Greeks surrounded us, pressing inwards. Ship after ship capsized; you couldn't see the water for wreckage and corpses. The beaches and shallows were all choked with bodies.

One by one, we tried to slink away. But the Greeks were like fishermen with a great haul of tunny netted and trapped – stabbing and smashing our men with broken oars, pieces of wreckage, whatever came to hand. The sea was filled with screams and groaning, until at last night fell and hid the scene. I could talk for a week, and still not tell you all I saw. But one thing is sure: never before have so many thousands died on a single day.[10]

Even Herodotos, summing up, sounds like a Headmaster announcing some victory in an inter-school match, and trying unsuccessfully to be fair to both sides:

The battle couldn't have ended any other way: the Greeks fought with good order and discipline, and kept to their positions, whereas the barbarians were disorganised and seemed to have no proper plan of action. Even so, they fought very bravely that day – far better than they'd done previously off Euboia. Every one of them fought as hard as he could, for fear of Xerxes, believing that the king was watching him alone.[11]

This was the heritage of the Athenians who sailed for Sicily – a heritage still treasured in Greece today, where Salamis, Thermopylae and Marathon are mentioned as we would talk of Trafalgar or Dunkirk. But unfortunately the fleet that reached Sicily was not so successful. The generals disagreed, and a great deal of time was wasted in pointless skirmishes, while the Sicilians, realising that a final showdown was inevitable, quietly made their preparations in the Great Harbour at Syracuse:

Remembering what they had learned in earlier sea-fights, they began making improvements in their ships. They shortened and strengthened the prows, and reinforced the beams that projected from them. These they also supported with buttresses 3 metres long, running down through the sides of the ships. They knew that the Athenian ships were not similarly strengthened, but had light prows suitable for a different method of fighting – not attacking prow to prow, but rowing round the enemy ships and ramming them from the side. Since the battle was to be fought in the Great Harbour, where the ships would be crowded together, the Syracusans hoped that their new tactics would bring them victory. They planned to charge prow to prow, and use their strengthened rams to smash in the enemy's bows, which were too flimsy and unprotected to withstand such thick, solid timbers. The Athenians would be trapped by the narrowness of the harbour, unable either to sail round them or move out of line to attack – the two manoeuvres they knew best.

This plan of battle turned to advantage what had before seemed a lack of skill on the part of Syracusan steersmen: ramming prow to prow was a manoeuvre they were good at, and could use again and again. Once it began, the Athenians would have no line of retreat except to the land, which was too close, and largely in Syracusan hands in any case. They thought that once the Sicilians controlled most of the harbour, and the Athenians began to get the worst of it, they would mass together in a narrow space, and so run foul of each other. And in fact that is just what happened; the Athenians were bunched together and unable to escape, whereas the Syracusans had command of the open sea, and could draw back and charge again from there whenever they wanted.[12]

When it came to the battle, these tactics and preparations, and a certain amount of over-confidence on the Athenian side, gave the Syracusans a great victory:

The Syracusans divided their fleet: some were sent to guard the harbour-entrance, and the rest were stationed all round it in a circle, so that they could attack the Athenians from all sides at once. They positioned their land forces as a second line of attack, in case any Athenians reached the shore.

The Athenians sailed up to the harbour barrier, and by force of numbers broke through the line of ships barring their way. But once they were inside the harbour the whole Syracusan fleet attacked them from all sides at once. No battle was ever greater or fiercer. The sailors on both sides were as eager to row hard against the enemy as the steersmen were to outdo each other in skill and alertness. The soldiers on the ships waited in good order, keeping to their positions; they were determined that when ship tangled with ship, their military skill would match their colleagues' seamanship.

The two fleets together came to nearly 200 ships. They were jammed so tightly together in the narrow harbour that there was no opportunity for ramming or breaking back for a charge. There were frequent collisions, ship fouling ship as they attacked or fell back from one another. While two ships bore down on each other, the soldiers on deck showered their opponents with spears, stones and arrows. When they met, there was fierce hand-to-hand fighting as each crew tried to board the other ship.

Often, because of the cramped space, a ship had no sooner rammed its opponent than it was rammed itself. On several occasions two or more ships attacked the same enemy, and became entangled; steersmen frequently had to out-manoeuvre several enemy ships at once. The crashing and splintering of ship against ship caused great confusion, and made it impossible to hear the orders shouted by the officers. (The Athenians were telling their men that their only chance of reaching home safely was to batter their way out of the harbour.

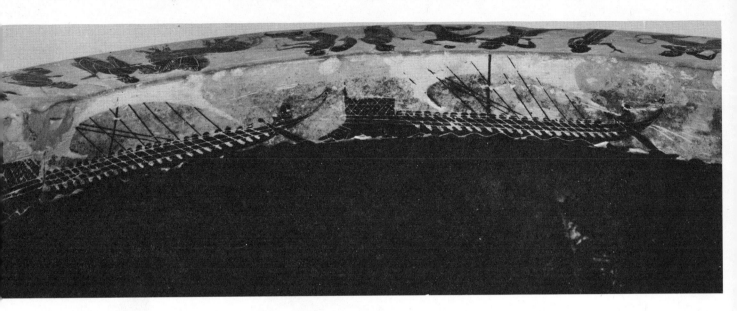

In this vase-painting one war-galley is shown just about to ram another. It shows clearly how vulnerable the rowers were to an attack along the ship's side.

The Syracusans and their allies were shouting to each other that if they could only cut off the Athenians' retreat, they would win a glorious victory that would bring credit on the whole of Sicily.)

At last, after many hours' fighting, the Syracusans did succeed in routing the Athenian fleet, and with eager shouts of excitement and encouragement drove them back to the shore. Many of the sailors had been killed at sea; the survivors rushed ashore in panic, and the Athenian ground-troops, with one concerted groan of despair, turned and ran as well. Some hurried to defend the ships, or guard what was left of their camp, but the majority were only anxious to save their own skins by flight.

The battle had been long and hard, and many ships and men had been lost on both sides. The victorious Syracusans gathered up the bodies of the dead, and salvaged what they could of the wreckage; then they sailed back to the city and put up a trophy. The Athenians were so crushed by the disaster that they never even thought of asking permission to gather up their dead or salvage their wrecked fleet. Their one thought was to wait for night, and then run for their lives.[13]

The sea gives, and the sea takes away. The Greeks have always been one of the great maritime nations, and their achievements as traders and sea-fighters are second to none. Nevertheless, there must have been times – after Syracuse, for example – when they wished they'd listened to the sour advice of Hesiod, who (untypically for a Greek) felt uneasy on the sea, and preferred the comparative security of a farmer's life:

If sea-travel, however uncomfortable, is in your blood and you can't give it up, learn weather-sense instead. When the Pleiades run from cruel Orion and plunge into the misty sea, gales and winds of all kinds will be raging. That's the time to keep off the wine-dark sea, and work the land instead. Haul your vessel up on shore, and pack stones all round it, to keep it safe from rain-soaked winds. Pull out the bung, or rain will rot the timbers. Take all the tackle and fitting indoors. Fold the sails (the wings of your swift ship) and store them carefully. Hang the well-made steering-oar over the fireplace, and wait for a better season for sailing.[14]

This octopus-jar may have been brought back as a souvenir of dangers past. It was probably used for storing oil.

4 · Everyday life

Alexandrian 'Wanted' poster, *c.* 150 B.C.:

Hermon, also called Neilos, a slave belonging to Aristogenes son of Chrysippos, the Alabandan Ambassador to Alexandria, has run away. A native of Bambyce in Syria, he is about eighteen years old, of average height, clean shaven, of good appearance, with a dimpled chin, a mole on the left of his nose, and a scar on the left side of his mouth. Tattooed on his right wrist are two foreign letters. He took with him three bags of gold coins, ten pearls, and an iron neckband embossed with an oil-flask and strigils. He was wearing a cloak and a loin-cloth. *Rewards*: 3 talents of copper for bringing him back alive; 2 talents if he is arrested in a temple; 5 talents if he is shown to be hiding in the house of a rich man who can be taken to court. All information to the governor's secretaries.[1]

For all their intelligence and deep philosophical study, the Greeks saw nothing wrong with slavery. It was not until after Christ that enlightened men began to wonder if it was right for one man to own another as completely and unconditionally as a horse or a table.

In 430 B.C., in the district round Athens, there were between 80,000 and 100,000 slaves, out of a total population of about 300,000. Poor households had only one slave, or perhaps none at all; but rich men had many. On the next page is a list of the slaves sold off to pay a nobleman's debts in 414 B.C. Their value is given in drachmas. (It is difficult to give a value for Greek money. All we can say is that you could buy a loaf of bread for 1 obol, and there were 6 obols in a drachma. The current value of bread will give some idea of the prices paid for these slaves.)

Nationality	Value
Thracian female	165 dr.
Thracian female	135 dr.
Thracian male	170 dr.
Syrian male	240 dr.
Carian male	105 dr.
Illyrian male	161 dr.
Thracian female	220 dr.
Thracian male	115 dr.
Scythian male	144 dr.
Illyrian male	144 dr.
Colchian male	153 dr.
Carian male (young)	174 dr.
Carian infant	72 dr.
Syrian male	301 dr.
Maltese male	106 dr.
Lydian female	170 dr.[2]

It's easy to imagine the qualities that would put a slave's price up (the ability to read and write; patience; good temper; honesty), and perhaps even easier to guess what would bring it down again. In general the Greeks seem to have treated their slaves well – much better than the Romans or Southern Americans, for example. Slaves are mentioned in most of the extracts in this chapter – and usually in a friendly way, as though the relationship was a normal one, and not strained or restrictive. A visitor to Athens in about 420 B.C. makes this comment:

Slaves and the lower classes are treated very freely here. For example, no one beats a slave, or expects him to stand aside in the street to let him pass. The reason for this is simple: Athenians dress no better than their slaves, and you can hardly tell master and servant apart, so that if there was a law saying a man could beat his slave or his social inferiors, one would often beat an Athenian citizen in mistake for a slave.[3]

In the next century Demosthenes quotes this law:

If anyone sees a man ill-treating anyone else, man, woman or child, free or

Nursemaid and baby. This clay statuette shows a figure from the theatre.

slave, or doing them any harm at all, he should report him to the proper authorities.[4]

It seems that Hermon, the slave mentioned in our first extract, was something of an exception. The relationship between master and slave was often a close one, and it was not unusual for slaves to be set free after long or distinguished service. Herodotos quotes one case, that of Themistokles' slave who took Xerxes the all-important message at Salamis (page 51):

This man's name was Sikinnos. He was Themistokles' house-slave, and his children's tutor. Later on, when the Thespians were admitting new citizens, Themistokles granted him citizenship there, and set him up with a comfortable sum to live on.[5]

In Homer's poems, the citizens of captured towns, rich or poor, farmers or kings, were usually enslaved by their captors. But whatever their former rank, once they were enslaved they worked at the same domestic tasks as anyone else. Here they are doing ordinary housework:

The lady Eurykleia, daughter of Ops and grand-daughter of Peisanor, called out to the slaves: 'Get to work now, girls! There's no time to waste! Some of you start sweeping and sprinkling the floors, and put purple rugs on all the chairs. While they're doing that, others can sponge the tables down, and clean the mixing-bowls and all the inlaid silverware. The rest of you, go to the well and fetch water. Be as quick as you can; today is a holiday, and our noble guests will be here soon.'

As soon as she'd finished the maids hurried to obey her. Twenty of them went to the well with its deep, dark water, and the rest bustled skilfully about the work inside the house. By the time the noblemen's servants arrived and began chopping wood, the maids had come back from the well, and the swineherd was with them, bringing for the feast the three best and fattest hogs in his herd.[6]

And here they are entertaining a guest:

Kirke's maidservants were busy in the great hall. There were four of them, wood-nymphs born of the springs and sacred rivers that flow down to the sea.

Mistress and slave. These tall jars, called lekythoi, *were often used for perfume, or placed in graves. This one is white (the Greek colour of mourning) with black figures.*

Above: *This clay group shows a number of slave-women kneading dough.*

Above right: *This carving, showing a girl putting clothes away, gives a good idea of the furniture in an ordinary Greek house. The objects hung on the wall include a basket and a mirror.*

Below right: *This drawing (from a vase-painting) shows a slave-girl fetching water from the well. She still holds the well-rope in her right hand.*

One of them put linen covers on the chairs, and spread fine purple rugs on top. Another placed beside each chair a silver table with a golden basket on it. The third mixed honey-sweet wine in a silver bowl, and set out the golden cups. The fourth brought water, and stirred up the fire under a huge three-legged cauldron. When the water was boiling, she sat me down in a bath-tub and poured in water from the cauldron, mixing it with cold to a comfortable heat, and pouring it over my head and shoulders till all the weariness was washed from my limbs. When she'd washed me and anointed me with soft olive-oil, she gave me a tunic and fine cloak to wear, and led me to one of the chairs, with their superb silver inlay. Food was brought, and the stately housekeeper invited me to fall to, and eat to my heart's content.[7]

Very often, of course, the mistress of the house not only supervised the work of the slaves, but did a good deal herself as well. Here is the charming description of Princess Nausikaa doing the laundry:

Nausikaa went to her father and said: 'Daddy dear, please will you let me have a mule-cart with good, strong wheels, so that I can take all the dirty clothes down to the river and wash them? You're a king, a leader of men, and it's only right that you should have clean clothes to wear to meetings. Two of your sons are married, but three are vigorous bachelors, always asking for clean clothes to go dancing in – and it's my job to provide them.'

That was the reason she gave. But her father realised that she was keeping the real reason – her own wedding-day – a secret locked in her heart. 'My dear child,' he said, 'you can have the mules and anything else you want. Go and get ready, and I'll tell the servants to harness up a wagon with good, strong wheels, and a canopy on top.'

He gave his orders, and the slaves brought out a mule-cart and harnessed up the mules. Nausikaa fetched all the best clothes down from the store-room and loaded them into the polished wagon, while her mother packed a basket with all sorts of delicious food, and a goatskin bottle of wine. Then Nausikaa climbed into the cart, and the queen gave them a golden flask of olive-oil, to anoint themselves when the work was done.

Nausikaa took the whip and the polished reins, and flicked the mules to go. They moved off eagerly, hooves clattering on the stones, taking their mistress and the clothes down to the river; and her maids went with her.

When they came to the great river, and its never-failing springs of clear water bubbling up to wash clean even the dirtiest clothes, they unyoked the mules and sent them off along the bank of the echoing river, where the grass was sweetest. Then they took armfuls of clothes from the cart and carried them to the river, making a game out of treading them down in the dark water. When all the dirt and stains were washed away, they spread the clothes out on the seashore, just above the line of pebbles thrown up by the sea. Then they bathed, anointed themselves with soft olive-oil, and sat on the river-bank to eat their dinner while they waited for the sun to dry the clothes. When they'd finished eating, mistress and maids threw off their heavy head-dresses and began to play with a ball.[8]

This pleasant, simple life was very much to Greek taste. Five centuries after Homer, Aristophanes' description of happiness is just as gentle and pastoral:

There is nothing else that gives me pleasure
Like a field just newly-sown,
When the gods in heaven send us rain,
And when a neighbour says:
'Come in, dear friend, and take a drink with us,
While this fine shower comes down
And God is helping us to grow the crops –
Come in, do please say yes!
Wife, put some beans in to cook, and find some cakes
And figs for us to eat;
And send a kitchen-maid to call the slaves in from
The yard: it's far too wet
For them to go on hoeing weeds and pruning vines –
Let's give them a treat
As well!' And someone else puts in: 'No, wait!
Don't start your feasting yet.
I'll go and get those pheasants that I bagged
The other day, and fetch some cream
As well – and four plates of hare, if I remember right.
They're in the larder now,
Unless our tabby's had them first: last night
I heard her bumping around inside the larder. But if
There's any left, I vow
We'll all enjoy it. Go and fetch it, slave;
Bring three to us, and take the rest
In to my father – oh yes, and ask the gardener
For a green bay bough
To flavour this dear lady's stew: and please
Be sure and get the best!
And while you're on the way, invite
The neighbours all to join us. How
Gracious heaven is towards us,
Blessing all our crops with rain
And bringing golden harvest nearer.'[9]

Banqueting scene. The wide, flat cups were called skyphoi. *They were held in the flat of the hand, and often beautifully painted. The photo on page 41 shows the inside of one.*

Notice how the food is basically vegetarian: pheasant is clearly a special luxury. Most people made do with a simple diet of bread, fruit, cheese and vegetables, eked out with meat or fish when they could get it.

Greek food was much more highly seasoned than ours. When Athens was besieged during the Peloponnesian War, one of the greatest hardships was that imports of Megarian garlic stopped. And how many of us could face a drink like this one, served to King Nestor by the Lady Hekamede?

First she set in front of them a fine polished table with decorated legs. On this she placed a bronze dish containing onion, barley-meal and yellow honey. Then she fetched the superb drinking-goblet Nestor had brought from home. It was studded with gold, and had four handles, each with twin supports underneath, and a pair of doves on top, facing each other as they fed. Anyone else would have found it hard to lift when it was full, but old Nestor could pick it up easily.

Hekamede poured Pramnian wine into this goblet, and stirred in the onion, barley-meal and honey. Then she grated goat's-milk cheese over it with a

63

This carving shows part of a sacrifice, involving bread, wine and a cockerel. Once the sacrifice was over, the feast could begin.

bronze grater, and sprinkled it with white pearl-barley. When everything was ready she invited them to drink.[10]

Once you'd got *that* down, things did improve a little:

A maid brought water in a fine golden ewer, and poured it into a silver bowl so that they could wash their hands. Then she placed a polished table beside them, and the stately housekeeper waited on them herself, serving them with all the good things she had to offer. Another slave brought a great dish filled with all kinds of sliced meats, and set in front of them a golden drinking-goblet, which the wine-steward hurried over to fill for them.[11]

Wine was one of the most important parts of a Greek meal. At a banquet the food would often be hurried through, so that the main part, the *symposion* or 'drinking-together', could begin. While the wine flowed, civilised conversation and cleverly-worded toasts were the order of the day. There might even be a cabaret:

A slave went to the king's apartments to fetch the hollow lyre, while others cleared a space for the dancers, and settled everyone round it in a circle. The slave came back with Demodokos' sweet-sounding lyre, and the minstrel went into the middle of the floor. Round him gathered a group of expert dancers, young men in the first bloom of youth. As he played, they began to dance, and all the watching guests marvelled at their skill and elegance.[12]

Sometimes the guests themselves joined in a drinking-song, like this one by Alkaios:

Let's start our drinking *now* – no time
To wait while they light the lamps.
There's a finger of daylight left,
So lift down the goblets, slave!
Lord Dionysos gave us wine
To ease our cares away.
Mix two parts water, one part wine,
And let's drink till morning comes![13]

But most often it would be talk, discussion and argument, lasting

Opposite: *Scenes from aristocratic life. This vase shows some episodes from the* Odyssey: *hunting, fighting, dining. Notice the griffins on the lowest band.*

A flute-player and dancers (or dancing guests). The flute is tied round the player's head, to leave both hands free.

most of the night. Strangers were particularly welcome: for in an age when there were no newspapers or other mass media, visitors from foreign parts were an important source of news.

The following story from Herodotos gives an idea what Greek banquets could be like at their most extravagant – and also the sort of thing that happened if the wine was too strong. Usually, as Alkaios says, it was diluted with one part wine to two of water; if this proportion was changed, things could easily get out of hand...

Kleisthenes had a daughter called Agariste, and he was anxious to marry her to the finest man in the whole of Greece. So during the Olympic Games, shortly after winning a crown in the four-horse chariot-race, he had a public announcement made that anyone who thought himself good enough to become Kleisthenes' son-in-law should present himself at Sikyon before sixty days were up. In one year from then, Kleisthenes would formally celebrate the wedding.

A great crowd of suitors came – everyone in Greece with a family or

A greedy slave (clay statuette showing a figure from comedy).

reputation to be proud of. Kleisthenes kept them busy with wrestling and racing, and built an arena specially for this purpose.

When the sixty-day period was over, and all the suitors had arrived, Kleisthenes began his enquiries. First he asked each of them his name and place of origin. Then he spent a whole year examining them, and finding out about their abilities, upbringing, temper and way of life. His method was to interview each of them individually and in the others' company, and give the younger ones tests in gymnastics. But the supreme test was their behaviour at meal-times: for throughout their stay Kleisthenes entertained them very lavishly and expensively.

The suitors from Athens came out best in all this testing, and best of *them* was Hippokleides son of Tisander. Kleisthenes liked him not only for his own abilities, but also because he was related to one of the oldest families of Corinth.

At last the day came for Kleisthenes to announce the name of his chosen son-in-law, and celebrate the marriage. 100 oxen were sacrificed, and all the people of Sikyon were invited to join the suitors at a banquet. After dinner the suitors competed with each other in poetry and public speaking, and as the evening wore on, Hippokleides, who was doing better – and drinking more – than anyone else, asked the flute-player to play for him, and began to dance.

Hippokleides thought his own dancing was magnificent, but Kleisthenes wasn't quite so pleased – especially when Hippokleides called for a table and climbed up on to it. First he did a Spartan dance, then some Athenian ones, and ended up by standing on his head and waving his legs in the air.

The Spartan and Athenian dances were bad enough, but the leg-waving was too much for Kleisthenes, who lost his temper and said: 'Hippokleides, you've just danced away your marriage.'

'So what?' said Hippokleides. 'See if Hippokleides cares!'

This answer soon became a proverb – but Kleisthenes married his daughter to Megakles, another of the suitors from Athens.[14]

Both Hippokleides and Kleisthenes, in different ways, were guilty of the worst social sin a Greek could commit: 'going too far'. But Hippokleides was the worse of the two: even his friends in Athens would have been shocked to hear of such behaviour, particularly in a stranger's house. The Greeks liked order, discipline and self-control. 'A place for everything, and everything in its place' was a saying they would have appreciated. Showing-off of the wrong sort was frowned on. Even their houses had to be simple and functional:

Furniture-moving. Furniture was often stored, not left in a room, and only brought out when needed.

Although public buildings in fifth-century Athens were magnificently and lavishly decorated, no private citizen owned a better house than anyone else. The houses even of Themistokles, Miltiades and the other great men of their day, were no bigger or more expensive than their neighbours'; public buildings, on the other hand, were as fine then as they are now. Consider for example the Gateway to the Akropolis, the Docks, the Arcades, the Harbour, and all the other places that bring distinction on the city.[15]

Some Greeks carried their passion for tidiness rather too far. The orderliness of *this* nobleman's house is just a little over-done:

Our house is not decorated in an ornate manner; each room is built the right shape and size for whatever is to go in it, and you can tell the purpose of each room just by looking at it. The master bedroom, for example, in the securest part of the house, contains the most valuable carpets and furniture; the driest rooms are used as grain-stores; the coolest rooms store wine; the brightest rooms contain the ornaments and furniture that are seen to best advantage in daylight. The living-quarters are carefully planned to be cool in summer, warm in winter; the house is designed so that we get maximum sunlight in winter, maximum shade in summer.

Our furniture, too, is placed where it will be of most use. Objects required for sacrifice are all collected together; my wife's best clothes, and my own armour and best clothes, are kept with the bed-linen; clothes for male and female slaves are kept in the appropriate rooms. Another store is for weapons, and another for wool-carding equipment; in another are the kitchen utensils, in another serving-dishes, in another bath-utensils; in another the baking-dishes are kept, and in another the cutlery and table-settings. Everything is carefully separated into things needed for special occasions and things used every day. Each month's stores and supplies are kept separately from the entire year's stock; in this way there is less danger of running out of anything without noticing.

The things each slave uses every day for cooking, baking or spinning, are kept by the individual slaves, and they are shown how to put them away and keep them safe. But everything used less often, for banquets or for entertaining guests, we leave in the charge of our housekeeper. She knows the place of each object and keeps written accounts, remembering who used each object last, and making sure it's returned to its proper place as soon as she gets it back.[16]

The Erechtheion on the Akropolis — one of the best-preserved buildings from the 'classical' period of Athens.

There speaks a man who loves organisation! His neighbours probably thought him a little odd: certainly he comes near to breaking the golden rule 'all things in moderation'. Any aspect of a person's character is all right in proportion, but becomes ridiculous or even dangerous if it's exaggerated. The people in Greek tragedy often 'go too far' – Antigone, for example, (page 79), pushes obedience to her conscience to the point where she seems stubborn, almost pig-headed.

But at least Antigone 'went too far' in something of real importance. On this page and the next are descriptions of two people who exaggerated more ordinary characteristics — types we could still easily meet today. The photos, too, show that in other ways the Ancient Greeks were very like ourselves.

The skinflint

When a servant breaks a plate or a jug, he stops the man's wages till it's paid for; when his wife drops a farthing he moves all the furniture aside, pulls back the cupboards and sofas, and burrows under the carpets. He won't let you walk across his land, or eat a fig out of his garden; you mustn't even touch olives or dates that have fallen on the ground. He examines his fences daily to make sure no one's interfered with them, and he won't let his wife lend anyone salt, or lampwick, or herbs, or onions, or barley, or garlands, or offerings. 'Small things they may be,' he says, 'but over a year they begin to add up.'

The superstitious man

He's terrified of anything remotely to do with the gods. He won't stir out of his door until he's washed his hands and sprinkled his head with holy water – and even then he keeps a bay-leaf in his mouth for good luck. If a cat runs in front of him, he won't move until he's thrown three stones across the road, or someone else has gone past ahead of him. When he passes the smooth stones at crossroads he sprinkles them with olive-oil, falls on his knees and kisses them before continuing his journey. If a mouse eats a hole in one of his corn-sacks, he goes to a wise-woman to ask what he ought to do; and if she says: 'Get it mended, of course!' he's not satisfied, but goes and makes a special sacrifice against bad luck. If he hears an owl he always says: 'Athene's greater!' before going on. On dates with a 4 or a 7 in them, he sets his slaves to boil wine, and goes out to buy myrtle, sacrificial cakes and incense; then he comes back, and spends the day garlanding the statues of the household gods. If he sees a statue of Hekate at a crossroads, especially one garlanded with garlic-leaves, he

Grumpy old man with basket (clay statuette showing a figure from comedy).

Terracotta group showing two ladies gossiping. It was probably intended as a bedroom or living-room ornament.

hurries away to wash his hair; then he hires a prophetess to make a purification-ceremony with a puppy or a bunch of lilies. If he sees a madman or an epileptic he shivers, and spits into his own bosom.[17]

In general the Greeks were pleasant, hard-working people, proud of their country and certain that their system of government and way of life were the best in the world. Perikles, a leading Athenian statesman, summed up what the people of *his* city thought best in themselves:

We like beautiful things, but don't spend a fortune on them; we like studying,

Perikles. This style of portrait-bust seems to have been popular—compare Themistokles (page 32). Perikles was nicknamed 'The Olympian'—and the sculptor here seems to have tried to give him some of the dignity and severity of Zeus.

but it doesn't make us soft. A wealthy man treats his money as something to use, not something to boast about. No one looks down on a poor man, unless he's too lazy to try and help himself.

Our people are as interested in public as in private life. No one puts his own affairs before those of the state – or if he does, we regard him as a useless citizen. Before we do anything we discuss it thoroughly and in public, believing that talk is no hindrance to action, but that action without prior discussion is dangerous.

In our personal lives we welcome comparison with anyone in the world. We make friends by doing favours, not receiving them. If you've helped someone you feel well-disposed towards them, and want to keep the friendship up; but favours received are like debts hanging round your neck, waiting to be paid off. When Greeks help their friends it is out of generosity of spirit, not because of what they hope to get out of it.[18]

5 · The theatre

No one really knows how or when Greek drama began. The first public performance in Athens was in 534 B.C. From then on, for 150 years, between twenty and thirty new plays were put on every year – a record no other city has ever equalled. Only a small number of these plays survive: seven tragedies by Aischylos, seven by Sophokles, nineteen by Euripides, and eleven comedies by Aristophanes. Some of them are counted among the greatest plays of all time.

The history of Greek drama begins with Dionysos, the god of wine and laughter, dancing and festivals. At the great Spring Festival in

This carving shows Dionysos, god of drama, with some of his servants in front of what may well be the stage-building in a theatre. Notice the masks worn by some of the figures on the right.

his honour, everyone sang hymns and songs, and went in procession round his shrines in the city. The hymns were probably like this one, from Euripides' *The Bacchae*:

> From the holy mountain-passes
> And the glens of far-off Asia
> We have come, lord Dionysos:
> Come to dance the sacred dances,
> Filled with love and holy joy.
>
> Who is listening? Who is stirring?
> No one must disturb the dancing,
> Break the rhythm of our singing
> As we raise our hymn together
> To our master Dionysos.
>
> Happy the man who loves the gods;
> He delights his soul with dancing
> In the glens of the holy mountain.
> Thyrsos* in hand, crowned with ivy,
> He dances to honour Dionysos,
> Full of the joy of the festival.
>
> Come and dance, all you who hear us;
> Come and worship Dionysos.
> Crown your heads with sacred vine-leaves,
> Raise on high the sacred pine-torch –
> Come and dance! Your god is here.[1]

The lower band on this vase shows a flute-player and some satyrs. (Satyrs were the drunken followers of Dionysos. Several of the plays at each drama-festival used satyrs as the chorus.)

Because it was important to keep evil spirits at bay, men were placed at various points on the route, to make fun of the processions as they passed by. In this way any jealous gods who saw the processions would think them ridiculous and unimportant, and leave them in peace.

Greek comedy probably grew out of this mockery. The following extract from Aristophanes' *Peace* shows what it was like. Aristophanes is poking fun at three rival poets.

*The thyrsos was a wooden staff carried by Dionysos' worshippers.

Muse, please reject all this warfare, and sing
For our poet alone; come, and bring
Us enjoyment, sweet laughter and song,
Wine, dancing and pleasure all festival long.
But if Karkinos asks you
To join him, dear Muse,
That's one of the tasks you
Must simply refuse –
For he's past it, old-fashioned and bad.
What plays has this genius written?
Not one with a morsel of wit in.
The Dwarves, The Quails, The Long-necked Cranes,
It Never Pours Here, but it Rains –
One chorus was nice,
From a play called *The Mice,*
Till a cat ate it up in rehearsal – how sad!

All experienced poets soon learn
That as soon as the swallows return
To the woods, and the whole world rejoices,
It's time with the Muses to lift up our voices.
But if Morsimos begs you
For help, dearest Muse,
His plays are just dregs you
Would never once choose
To put in for a contest or crown.
With his brother to help him, he wrote
The following dramas of note:
The Greedy Pigs, The Harpies, Filthy Swine,
The Death of Fish, Why Old Maids always Whine –
How can poets like these
Fight Aristophanes
Without making men mock them, and drive them from town?[2]

From simple beginnings Greek drama progressed very quickly. It soon became customary for each festival to include a dramatic competition, and large theatres were built all over Greece, some of them for as many as 20,000 people. Authors and actors were respected men,

The Theatre of Dionysos, at the foot of the Akropolis in Athens. It was here that many of our surviving Greek plays were first performed.

and the rich fought for the privilege of financing plays. The great dramatic festivals soon became the most important occasions in a city's year.

But these festivals still had a religious theme, and most of the plays were about the gods and their dealings with mankind. In comedy the gods are often mocked, in an affectionate way. In Aristophanes' *The*

Head of Dionysos (from a coin).

Right: *A scene from comedy. A reveller (possibly Herakles) is knocking on a door in the middle of the night. Notice the slave-girl's lamp, and the expression on her face.*

Frogs, for example, the main character is Dionysos himself. He has pressing reasons for visiting the Underworld; but unfortunately, as well as being fat, he is stupid and cowardly. So, to give himself courage, he dresses up as the hero Herakles, who went down to Hell once before, and lived to tell the tale. Dionysos and his slave eventually reach the door of Pluto, king of the Underworld; but their reception there is not at all the sort of thing a god has a right to expect.

DIONYSOS Ah, here we are. . .Pluto's palace. What's the best way to knock, d'you think? How do they knock on doors in these parts?

SLAVE Oh, any way you like! Get on with it.

DIONYSOS Right. (*hammering on the door*) All right, you lot! Anyone in?

PORTER (*opening the door fiercely*) 'oo is it?

DIONYSOS (*nervously*) Er. . .Herakles. . .Herakles the Strong.

PORTER So it's you again, is it? You 'orrible little man, thought you'd come back and see how we was doing, did you? AND STAND UP STRAIGHT WHEN I'M TALKING TO YOU! Runs off with our guard-dog, then comes back to laugh

Comic actors. Their costumes are grotesquely padded. At the top left-hand side the artist has drawn a comic mask.

at us! A right little joker – AND GET YOUR HAIR CUT! Well, I've got news for you. We've been waiting for you. Our gorgons'll 'ave you, sharpish, AND I wouldn't like to be you when they've finished with you. You'll be on tortures so fast, your feet won't touch the ground. WHAT WAS THAT? You got anything to say, my lad, you keep quiet about it, or I'll 'ave you. . .I'll 'ave you as far as Tartaros and back.

DIONYSOS But. . .

PORTER WAIT FOR IT! I'll tell you when to speak! (*He goes.* DIONYSOS *slumps*)

SLAVE Sir, sir, what's the matter?

DIONYSOS I've. . .er. ..had an accident.

SLAVE Why don't you clear off while you've got the chance?

DIONYSOS (*in anguish*) You don't understand. . .I've had an *accident*. Give me a sponge, quick.

SLAVE Where d'you want it?

DIONYSOS Put it on my heart. There.

SLAVE Good lord! Is *that* where you keep your heart?

DIONYSOS It. . .er. . .slipped a bit in the excitement.

SLAVE Huh! A right little Herakles *you* are![3]

Clearly none of this is meant to be taken seriously. The Greeks would have been very surprised by our idea that it is blasphemy to make fun of god.

But things were very different in tragedy. Here the gods are grim, unsmiling powers who deal in Justice, Obedience and Destiny, whose word is law and whose anger must be avoided at all costs.

The story of Antigone shows what happened when these powers were defied. Antigone had two brothers, Eteokles and Polyneikes. Polyneikes was a traitor, and attacked his native land. Eteokles defended it, and the two brothers killed each other in single combat. Kreon, king of the city, decreed that the hero Eteokles was to be buried with full military honours, but the traitor Polyneikes was to be left unburied on the plain, to rot.

Antigone disagreed. The king's law was not the gods' law. Heaven says that brothers must be honoured, whatever crimes they commit, and whatever decrees are made by a mortal king. So she buried Polyneikes' body, and was arrested and brought before Kreon.

KREON Antigone. . .Antigone, look at me. . .
 Do you admit this crime, or deny it?
ANTIGONE Yes, I admit it. Why should I deny it?
KREON Did you know of my law forbidding it?
ANTIGONE After your proclamation, all Thebes knew.
KREON You knew — and still you dared to disobey?
ANTIGONE Yes. For it was not Zeus who made this law,
 Or Justice, who lives with the gods below —
 It was you, a mortal. And I thought
 No mortal's proclamation strong enough
 To over-rule the gods' unwritten laws:
 Laws not made to last a day or a year,
 But for ever; laws no mortal man
 Could ever make me break. The penalty
 Was death — I knew that. But I also knew,
 Without needing your proclamation to tell me,
 That I would have to die one day, soon or late.
 And can you not see how I long for death?
 My life is a sea of pain: when death comes

I shall bear it easily. What I could not bear
Would be the thought that I had left my brother,
My own mother's son, to rot unburied.
Does that seem foolish to you? If so,
Consider this: which is more foolish, my love
For my brother, or your law calling it a crime?
CHORUS She is proud and stubborn, her father's daughter.
She has never learned to give way to troubles.
KREON She'll give way! Great pride brings a great fall.
The hardest iron melts in a little fire;
A little bridle tames the proudest horse —
Antigone will give way. No one will say
The slave was greater than the master here.
She must answer for two crimes: first, she broke
The law I had proclaimed; second, she laughs
At Justice, now she is captured, and boasts
Of what she did. Am I the king of Thebes
Or is she? I shall punish her
As I proclaimed I would. She is my niece —
But even if she was my own daughter
She could not break the law and go scot-free.
ANTIGONE The penalty was death. Is that enough?
KREON I will be satisfied with your death, yes.
ANTIGONE Why delay, then? Why not kill me now?
We have no more to say to one another.
I have buried my brother, and won, by that,
The greatest glory I could have wished for.
I know that everyone in Thebes agrees —
Only fear of you prevents them speaking out.
Tyrants hear only what they want to hear.
KREON No! You are wrong! No one in Thebes agrees.
ANTIGONE They do — but they see you, and say nothing.
KREON I tell you you're alone. Are you not ashamed?
ANTIGONE Ashamed? Ashamed of loving my own brother?
KREON And Eteokles, the enemy he killed —
Was he not your brother too?
ANTIGONE He was.
KREON And don't you see how you dishonour him?

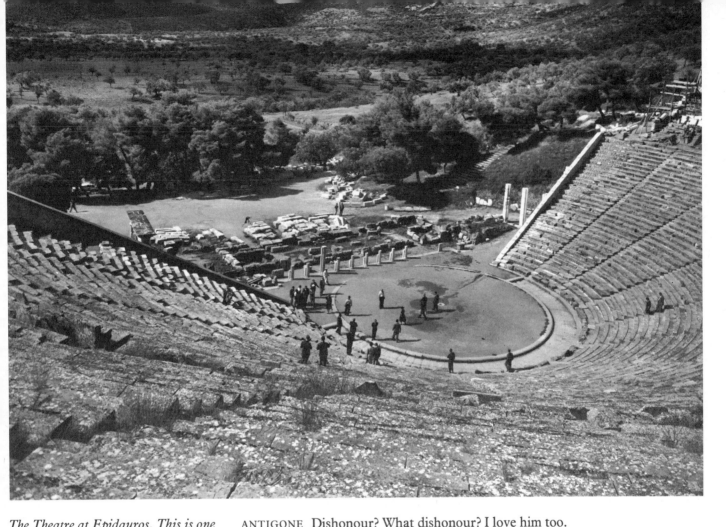

The Theatre at Epidauros. This is one of the largest and best-preserved of all Greek theatres. It is part of a healing-shrine of the god Asklepios.

ANTIGONE Dishonour? What dishonour? I love him too.

KREON You love him second to a criminal.

ANTIGONE It was his brother, not a criminal, who died.

KREON Yes: attacking Thebes, while he defended it.

ANTIGONE But now they are dead, we must love them both.

KREON Love them both? A traitor and a hero?

ANTIGONE Their death is the same, and makes them equal.

KREON An enemy can never be loved, not even in death.

ANTIGONE I was born to love, not hate, my brothers.

KREON Love them, then! Go down to hell, and love them there!
No woman will rule Thebes while I am king![4]

Antigone is led away to her death. But the gods are watching, and before long Kreon himself is punished, for daring to oppose their laws. His wife and son are killed, and he is left alone, to live the rest of his life in misery.

In Greek tragedy the vengeance of the gods is always swift, terrible and unavoidable. In Euripides' *The Bacchae* Dionysos – no longer the fat coward of *The Frogs* – takes a horrible revenge on Pentheus, king of Thebes, who has refused to believe in his divine power. All the women of Thebes have taken to the mountains, filled with religious madness. Dionysos asks Pentheus if he would like to see them at their rites. Not realising what is in store for him, Pentheus agrees. A servant goes with them up the mountainside; after a while he stumbles back, full of horror, to tell the audience what happened:

We left Thebes behind, crossed the river,
And made for the foothills of Kithairon,
Pentheus and I – for I went with my master –
And the stranger who was leading us.
We came to a grassy glade, and sat down,
Keeping tongues and feet quiet as mice:
We wanted to see, not to be seen.
The valley was walled by cliffs, and watered
By a stream – and there, in the shade of the pines,
We saw the Bacchae sitting quietly, their hands
Busy at pleasant tasks. Some were twining fresh ivy
Round a thyrsos that had lost its crown;
Others, happy as foals freed from the yoke,
Were singing in honour of Dionysos.
All this I saw clearly; but Pentheus was doomed,
And could see nothing. He said: 'Stranger,
From here these Bacchae of yours are invisible.
If I climbed a tall pine, up on the hill,
I could see every detail of their rites.'
Then, before our eyes, the stranger performed
A miracle. He took hold of the topmost branch
Of a tall pine where it brushed the sky,
And bent it down . . . down . . . down to the dark earth,

Tragic actor, carved in ivory. This figure is much later than the great period of Greek drama, but the pose and the expression are very like those of actors in classical times.

Arched like a bow or a curved wheel's edge,
Or like a perfect circle drawn with compasses:
That was how the stranger bent the tree –
No mortal man could have done it.
He sat Pentheus on the topmost branches,
Then set the tree upright again – gently
So as not to dislodge the king. The pine reared
Up to the sky, with Pentheus perched on top.
He could still see nothing – but now
He was clearly visible to the women below.
At first they did not notice him. But then, suddenly
I felt that the stranger was gone; and a voice
From the air – Dionysos, it must have been – cried:
'Look, women! Here is the man who mocked you,
Laughed at your rites, imprisoned me, your god.
He is in your hands – punish him!' As the god spoke
He sent a column of fire leaping from earth to sky.
The air grew still: grove, trees, forest beasts,
All silent. The women stood up, listening. . .
Then, when they heard the voice again,
On they came, swift as doves, through the grove,
Leaping from rock to rock beside the stream,
Filled with the breath of the god. When they saw
Pentheus, perched in his tree, their first thought
Was to knock him out of it by hurling rocks.
They climbed the towering cliff opposite,
And shot sharpened branches at him.
But it was useless: he was too high,
Sitting there helpless, terrified, out of reach.
Then his mother Agaue, the priestess, said:
'Stand round the tree, and grip it hard;
We must capture this climbing beast, before
It can reveal our ritual, and tell
Our secret dances.' The women obeyed her. . .
They set hands to the tree and ripped it
From the ground. Pentheus fell like a stone,
Screaming with terror: he knew his death
Was on him. His mother began the sacrifice;

83

When he saw her claws he lifted his face
And cried piteously, stroking her cheek:
'Mother! Don't hurt me! It's Pentheus. . .
Your son, your only son. Don't kill your own son!'
But Agaue's mouth was foaming; her eyes rolled
In her head; the Bacchic power was in her –
How could she recognise him? The others
Crowded round, tearing and ripping his flesh,
And the air was filled with noise: the Bacchae chanting,
And Pentheus screaming while his breath lasted.
Now his body lies scattered, at the cliff's foot
Or in dark thickets at the heart of the wood,
Where it will be hard to find. A man
Must learn to be humble and respect the gods.
I know that now: we have no greater gift,
And we must learn to use it.[5]

In scenes like this the message of Greek tragedy is made clear. Obedience to the gods is the only way to avoid disaster: resistance to fate only brings greater suffering. For the gods are all-powerful, and no man can understand or influence them. As Euripides wrote at the end of *The Bacchae*:

The gods follow no laws but their own:
What men hope for never happens,
And what they least expect occurs
By the will of heaven. So it was
With what has happened here.[6]

By late afternoon at the festival, when the audience had seen three tragedies in a row, they must have been feeling depressed and exhausted. Fortunately, the fourth play did bring some relief. It was a comedy, either about Dionysos' drunken followers the Satyrs, or dealing with ordinary events and people. For example, we have already mentioned Sokrates, the Athenian philosopher (Chapter 2, page 32). Here is how Aristophanes, his friend and contemporary,

Theatre-tickets (above), and a modern performance in the theatre at Delphi.

Vase-painting showing a scene from comedy. The actors' padded costumes and grotesque masks can be clearly seen.

made fun of him in *The Clouds*. An old man, Strepsiades, visits Sokrates' Think-shop to learn how to argue properly. The strange sights he sees there, and their even stranger explanations, make him wonder if he's come to the right place after all.

STUDENT For heaven's sake! Who's that hammering on the door?

STREPSIADES Me. Strepsiades.

STUDENT I wish you'd knock more *intellectually*. I had a brilliant thought just now, and nearly lost it altogether.

STREPSIADES I'm sorry. They don't tell us anything in the country. What sort of brilliant thought?

STUDENT Ah! Thoughts are private – except to *bona fide* students.

STREPSIADES Well, that's all right: I've come to sign on.

STUDENT Oh. All right, how's this for a brilliant thought – and mind you keep it to yourself. The other day Sokrates and Chairephon were trying to find out how many of its own feet a flea could jump.

STREPSIADES Which flea?

STUDENT The one that had just bitten Chairephon's eyebrow, of course. It jumped on to Sokrates' head.

STREPSIADES Oh. And how did he measure the distance?

STUDENT It was really very clever. He caught the flea, and stuck its feet in melted wax. . .gave it a pair of Persian slippers. When the wax hardened, he measured it, and hey presto!

STREPSIADES Goodness, what a brain!

STUDENT That's nothing compared to yesterday. . .when a lizard made him lose a really magnificent thought.

STREPSIADES What lizard? How?

STUDENT He was investigating the moon. . .making notes on its path through the sky.

STREPSIADES Well?

STUDENT Well, to do that he had to keep looking up. That's where the lizard came in.

STREPSIADES Came in? Where?

STUDENT On the roof, of course.

STREPSIADES I still don't get it.

STUDENT (*patiently*) Look: Sokrates is thinking. . .looking up. The lizard's on the roof. . .looking down. All at once, *bim*, *bam*! Sokrates gets an eyeful of droppings. . .end of thought.

STREPSIADES Oh, very clever. Quick, let me in! I must see him.

STUDENT Step this way. . .

STREPSIADES (*in amazement, as he enters*) Herakles! What on earth are those?

STUDENT What do they look like?

STREPSIADES Nothing on earth. What are they staring at the ground for?

STUDENT To work out what's underneath, of course.

STREPSIADES Good lord, that's easy. . .onions, turnips, carrots. . .! Hey, you lot, stop looking . . . I can let you have some, off the farm. (*looking the other way*) Golly, more of them! Why are they bent double like that?

STUDENT They're investigating the Underworld.

STREPSIADES Why are their bottoms stuck up in the air?

STUDENT Fundamental astronomy, of course.

STREPSIADES And who's that . . . up there in that balloon?

STUDENT The Prof.

STREPSIADES What prof?

STUDENT Sokrates.

STREPSIADES Sokrates? Quick, call him down for me!

STUDENT Call him yourself. I'm busy.

STREPSIADES Sokrates! Sok . . . rates! Sok-kee!

SOKRATES (*grandly, from the balloon*) 'Why call'st thou me, O mortal man?'

Sokrates.

STREPSIADES What are you doing up there?

SOKRATES 'I tread the air, and gaze upon the sun.'

STREPSIADES Can't you come down, and tell me what I want to know?

SOKRATES What *do* you want to know?

STREPSIADES How to get out of debt, for a start.

SOKRATES Is *that* all?

STREPSIADES Look, whatever your fee is, I'll pay it. I only want a couple of lessons.

SOKRATES Just a minute. (*as he brings the balloon down to earth*) You really are a genuine student?

STREPSIADES Of course I am.

SOKRATES All right, sit down there . . . on that sacred garden seat.

STREPSIADES (*sitting*) There.

SOKRATES Now, put this garland on.

STREPSIADES Why? Are you going to sacrifice me?

SOKRATES No, but I *am* going to sacrifice my principles, and *answer* a few questions for a change.[7]

In gentle comedy like this the characters are much more natural, more *human*, than in tragedy. It was such a popular style that later writers of tragedy took it up as well. Euripides' *Medea* is a good example. In this play the heroine is deserted and betrayed by her husband, who leaves her to marry another woman. Medea plans a terrible revenge. The gods play very little part in this story – in fact, except that Medea is a witch, a priestess with magical powers, it could easily be the plot of a modern play.

MEDEA I am trapped, surrounded by disaster
　　On every side. There is only one gleam
　　Of hope: Jason and his bride are doomed,
　　And all who love them will die with them.
　　There are so many ways I can kill them:
　　I can burn the palace round them, or creep
　　Into the bedroom where they lie entwined,
　　And let my knife drink their blood.
　　But both these ways are dangerous:
　　If I am seen in the palace, I will die,

And be cheated of my revenge. Poison is best:
I have used it before, and know its secrets.

And once I have killed them, where shall I go?
Who will take me in, and protect me
Against Jason's angry followers? No, no,
I must wait a little while. If I can find
A safe place to escape to, I will poison them;
But if there is nowhere in the world to hide,
I will gather up all my courage, and use
A sword on them. For they must die — all of them.
I am Medea, grand-daughter of the Sun;
How can they harm me, and not suffer for it?
I swear by Hekate, the dark goddess
I have known and honoured all my life,
That I will make this a bitter marriage,
Make Jason regret the day he injured me.[8]

Jason's new wife is murdered. But that is not the end of Medea's revenge, as Jason finds out when he bursts into the palace to find her for killing his bride.

JASON Where is that viper Medea — out here
    In the courtyard, or lurking in the palace?
    Wherever she hides, she will not escape:
    She can plunge deep into the Underworld,
    Or take wings and soar up to Heaven itself,
    But my guards will still find her,
    And punish her for what she has done today.
CHORUS Have you not heard what else has happened —
    The latest tragedy? Have they not told you yet?
JASON What tragedy? Is she planning to kill me too?
CHORUS Your sons are dead — by their own mother's hand.
JASON Woman, what are you saying? My sons — dead?
CHORUS They are dead. Their brief hour of life is ended.
JASON Where did she kill them? Out here, or inside?
CHORUS Open the palace doors, and you will see.

JASON   Guards! Quickly! Unbar the gates! Find their bodies –
And their murderess, whom I will repay with death!
(The guards rush to the gates. But suddenly Medea appears overhead in a chariot drawn by winged horses. Her dead sons are at her feet.)
MEDEA   I am here, Jason – here with your children.
If you have anything to say, say it now.

(With a cry of fury, Jason lunges at her with his sword.)
You cannot reach me: my grandfather the Sun
Has given me this chariot to protect me
And carry me out of your reach for ever.
JASON   You viper! Do you dare ask the Sun to help you –
You, the woman who murdered her own sons
And left their father childless, the woman
Detested by the gods and the whole human race?
Why did I ever bring you here, or marry you?
I cherished in my heart the pestilence
That was to destroy my life, the tigress
Even the monsters of hell are afraid to look on!
But my scorn is wasted on you: your ears
Are too full of the screams of your victims
For words of mine to move you. Go, now –
You have left me nothing but misery;
I have no wife to cherish, no hopes of children,
You have destroyed me, Medea – go . . . go!
MEDEA   I will not waste words answering you.
Zeus knows who is destroyer and who destroyed.
You thought you could scorn our marriage,
And you have been punished. Call me a viper,
A tigress, if you like – I have broken your heart
And taken the vengeance I longed for.
JASON   And you have broken your own heart as well;
My grief is your grief too.
MEDEA   My sons are dead;
Their father's tears are my only comfort.
JASON   O my sons, how your mother hated you!
MEDEA   No, my sons – your father's crimes destroyed you.
JASON   My crimes? Was it my hand that killed them?
MEDEA   No: it was your marriage, and your pride.

Tragic mask. This stone carving would have been far too heavy to wear. Real masks were usually made from cloth stiffened with resin.

JASON The gods will punish you.
MEDEA No: for they know who is really guilty.
JASON Is there no room in your heart for pity?
MEDEA None. I despise you, Jason.
JASON Well then, give me their bodies to bury,
  And leave Corinth. I will not keep you here.
MEDEA No: I will bury them myself.
JASON May the Furies destroy you for what you have done —
  And may avenging Justice . . .
MEDEA Why should the gods listen to you?
  You broke your oaths, and cheated those you loved.
JASON But it was not I who killed my own sons.
MEDEA Go inside. Go in and bury your wife.
JASON O my children! Let me touch them again!
  Let me kiss them, and caress them for the last time.
MEDEA No. You turned them away before:
  Why should you embrace them now?
JASON Medea, I beg you, let me touch them —
MEDEA No. You are wasting your breath.
JASON O Zeus, can you not hear her?
  She has murdered her own children,
  And still she will not let me touch them!
  I will mourn them for ever,
  Mourn for the sons I begot
  For their own mother to kill!
CHORUS High overhead, in Olympos,
  Lord Zeus looks after the affairs of men.
  The gods follow no laws but their own:
  What men hope for never happens,
  And what they least expect occurs
  By the will of heaven. So it was
  With what has happened here.[9]

The short extracts in this chapter can give very little idea of the real greatness of Greek drama. More than any of the works quoted in this book the plays should be read complete.* To whet your appetite, we

*A book list, including complete translations of all the plays quoted from in this chapter, is given on page 130.

The Theatre at Epidauros. This photo was taken from one of the side-entrances, through which the chorus came in procession. It gives a good idea of the huge size of the theatre.

give as our last extract the opening scene of Aristophanes' *Peace*. What sort of story could possibly follow *this*?

Scene: a farmyard, with a half-open stable door to one side. A slave hurries in, calling impatiently to someone offstage.

1st SLAVE Come on, where are you? Bring the beetle another pie!
   (The 2nd Slave staggers in with a huge dung pie.)

2nd SLAVE Here: you give it him, the filthy brute! Phew, what a stink! He certainly knows what he likes, this one . . .

1st SLAVE Shut up and get him another one – ass-dung this time.

2nd SLAVE What's happened to the one I brought just now? Don't tell me he's eaten it already?

1st SLAVE Eaten it? of course he has – rolled it into a ball and swallowed it down before you could blink. Go and mix up another lot.

2nd SLAVE Oh dear! Is there a bog-attendant in the house? I'm getting stunk to death up here.

1st SLAVE Get on with it – he's getting impatient. Says they're not round enough, either.

2nd SLAVE *(gloomily)* There's one thing, anyway: they won't catch me nibbling juicy bits out of *his* plates!

1st SLAVE For heaven's sake! Get mixing, can't you?

2nd SLAVE No! I tell you I've had enough.

1st SLAVE Pick up that pail and go.

2nd SLAVE You pick it up and go – to hell! *(to the audience)* Look, ladies and gentlemen, I put it to you: how can anyone do a job like this, with a sensitive nose like mine? Can you imagine a worse job? Fetching a dung-beetle his favourite food! A dog or a pig, they cause no trouble at all: drop it where you like, they always sniff it out. But not Lord Muck here: personal delivery service, he wants . . . keeps me slaving over a hot dung-pail all day long. *(Pause)* Here! What's he doing? He can't have finished, surely. Hang on, I'll take a look. *(peering into the stable)* Carefully, so he doesn't see me . . . *(recoiling)* Ugh! You filthy brute! Go on, guzzle away till you burst! You should see the way he gets down to it – just like a wrestler: flying jaw-locks, pastry cross-buttocks, the whole works! Whirling his feet round and round as though he was knitting a jumper! Ugh, what a filthy, greedy, nasty-smelling brute. You know what he reminds me of?

1st SLAVE Never mind that. Go and do him something to drink.

2nd SLAVE Oh, charming!

1st SLAVE Go on. I've got to stay here and tell this lot the plot. Listen, kiddies . . . ladies and gentlemen . . . *(whispering)* those at the front . . . *(shouting)* and those at the back! My master's gone mad: that's what it's all about. But not mad in the usual sort of way: not war-mad, like you lot. Very strange, it is. He stands there all day long staring at the sky, and shouting: 'Zeus! Hey Zeus! What's the game? Put down your brush: leave Greece alone, can't you?'

FARMER *(from inside)* O Zeus!

1st SLAVE There you are! Listen to this . . . you'll see . . .

FARMER Zeus, what are you trying to do to us? You'll look a real fool if you kill us all off, and starve yourself to death.

1st SLAVE There. Just the sort of thing I meant. And there's another symptom, too. When he first went round the bend, he suddenly announced: 'All right! I'm going up there to have a word with Zeus myself, in person!' So he got a pair of steps, and climbed up them, trying to get to heaven. Well, naturally he fell off . . . nearly broke his neck. And that's when he went and bought that thoroughbred beetle in there. Stinking, ugly brute! I have to feed it and groom it like a proper horse. He keeps coming in and stroking it, cuddling it and saying: 'Oh Pegasos! Dear old Peggy! Grow big and strong, and carry me up to Zeus on high!' – it's a proper tragedy just to hear him. *(Pause)* Just a minute . . . it's gone very quiet. What's he doing? I'd better have a look. *(looking in at the stable door)* Oh, my god! He's off now – halfway up to the Heaven on the wretched thing! Master! Come back! Help, someone! For heaven's sake, help!

(The farmer rides out of the stable on the back of the dung-beetle.)[10]

6 · Time off

Achilles brought out the prizes for the running race: the first prize was a fine silver mixing-bowl, holding six pints, the second a large, well-fed ox and the third half a talent of gold. Then Achilles stood up and announced: 'All contestants for the foot-race, come forward now.' The first to enter was Aias, a very quick sprinter, then the crafty Odysseus and finally Nestor's son, Antilochos, who was the fastest of the younger generation. They stood in a line and Achilles showed them where they had to turn.

Off they went, at full stretch right from the start. Aias took an early lead, but Odysseus was close behind him, so close that his feet were in Aias' tracks before the dust could settle and he was literally breathing down Aias' neck. Odysseus was running flat out and the shouts of the Greeks were a needless encouragement to his efforts.

Drawing of a footrace (from a vase-painting). The 'gym' part of 'gymnastics' originally meant 'naked'.

But as they were nearing the finish, Odysseus prayed silently to grey-eyed Athene: 'Hear me, goddess, and lend me speed.' Athene heard his prayer and his feet and hands were suddenly lighter. Then, just as they were finishing, Aias slipped – thanks to Athene – just where the ground was covered with dung, dropped by the cattle Achilles had sacrificed for Patroklos' funeral. His mouth and nostrils were full of the stuff. So Odysseus shot past him and carried off the silver bowl. Aias won the bull, and stood with his hands on one of its horns, spitting out lumps of muck. 'Damn it all,' he shouted, 'it was the goddess who tripped me up – that one who's always hanging round Odysseus; you'd think she was his mother.'

At which everyone roared with laughter.[1]

This race was one of the games organised by Achilles to celebrate the funeral of his friend Patroklos. A mixture of mourning and sprinting seems odd to us; but the Greeks regarded a strong body as a gift from the gods and saw nothing wrong in marking a solemn religious occasion with a display of athletics. The Olympic games are probably the best known example of this attitude. They were held at Olympia every four years in honour of Zeus and this next short piece of information is very telling:

Because the people of Elis were the organisers of the Olympic games, they had an agreement with the rest of the Greeks that their city was to remain sacred and free from attack; as a result, they were complete strangers to war and everything it entails.[2]

The modern Olympics have been held every four years since 1896 – except in 1916, 1940 and 1944.

But some of the details have stayed much the same. Practice methods, for instance:

Surely, if we were boxers, we would practise for days beforehand, trying out the punches and parries which we were going to use on the day; and to make it as real as possible, instead of the usual leather straps we would put on boxing-gloves, so that we could try out the punches at full strength without hurting anybody. And if we ran out of sparring partners, we should be so afraid of being defeated and laughed at that we would hang up a dummy and have a go

These are the ruins of the huge temple of Zeus at Olympia, still one of the most impressive sites in the whole of Greece.

at that. Or, failing all this, we would resort to shadow boxing by ourselves. How else can the art of self-defence be practised?[3]

A real fight is described by Homer, as another of the funeral events, and although this description comes from a time long before the first

Boxers (from a vase-painting). The 'gloves' consist of leather thongs wound round the hands and wrists. In later times these thongs were sometimes studded with lumps of metal.

Olympics were held, the time could equally well be the twentieth century A.D.:

Achilles now brought out the prizes for the boxing match: for the winner, a tough-looking mule, six years old and not broken in – which is a hard job with mules – and for the loser a two-handled cup. He then stood up and announced, 'My lords, men of the Greek army, I hope the two best boxers among you will now step forward to compete for these prizes: this mule for the man who, in our opinion, is favoured with victory by Apollo, and for the loser, this two-handled cup.'

The challenge was immediately answered by Epeios, a huge man who had skill as well as guts. He gave the mule a slap and said, 'Come on now, who's interested in winning a two-handled cup? You can forget the mule; she's mine.

I may not be the best warrior here – no one can be the best at everything – but I'll tell you what's going to happen to my opponent: I'm going to tear his flesh from his body and smash his bones to pulp. So I advise all his seconds to stand by, to carry him out of the ring when I have finished with him.'

There was complete silence. Then one man stood up, a well set-up fellow called Euryalos. His cousin Diomedes gave him a big hand and was obviously keen for him to win, helping him to get into his boxing kit and tying the leather straps round his hands. The two contestants then stepped into the middle of the ring, put up their fists and the fight began.

Soon their jaws were cracking horribly under the blows and sweat was pouring off their bodies. Suddenly, Epeios saw his chance and took it. Euryalos' concentration had flagged for a second and Epeios caught him a punch on the jaw that knocked his legs from under him. In fact, it was so fierce that it lifted him right off the ground, and he looked like one of those fish that leap out of the calm sea when it is ruffled by a breeze and then disappear again into the deep. Epeios generously helped him to his feet and his friends came crowding round. They had to drag him from the ring, spitting blood, his feet trailing behind him. He tried to keep his head straight on his shoulders, but he was almost unconscious, so that he had to be pulled along and his friends had to go and collect the two-handled cup themselves.[4]

The other Olympic events included wrestling, the long jump, the discus and the javelin. Our final extract from the Homeric games is of an event which never found its way into the ancient Olympics:

The next competition was putting the shot, which was itself the prize. It was a battered lump of pig iron that had once been a weapon in Eëtion's mighty hand. Achilles killed him and took this lump of iron on board ship with all Eëtion's other belongings. He now stood up and issued the usual invitation to the competitors. 'Gentlemen, if you win this contest you'll have enough iron to keep your farm supplied for five years. It won't matter how far you are from the nearest town, because none of your farmworkers will need to go there, not for iron anyway.'

Four competitors lined up, Polypoites, Leonteus, Aias and Epeios, who threw first. He took the shot in his hand, whirled it round and let go; and was greeted with hoots of laughter. Next was Leonteus and third Aias, who threw a good one, further than the other two. Last was Polypoites and his throw went way ahead of the rest; the distance between his and the others was as far as a

Throwing the discus.

cowherd can throw his stick, when he hurls it at his cattle to turn them. Everyone roared their congratulations and Polypoites' friends carried his prize off to the ships, a prize fit for a king.[5]

Of all the Olympic events, the one which carried the greatest prestige was the chariot race. For a start, it was exciting, and the margin of error for the charioteers was very small. But more than this, it was a snob event. Horses have always been expensive things to keep and the owners of chariot teams came decidedly from the upper crust of Greek society:

People were always talking about Alkibiades' racing stables and the number of chariots he had. No one, private citizen or king for that matter, ever entered seven chariots at the Olympic Games except him. According to Thukydides, he won first, second and fourth prizes and according to Euripides, the third prize; one can hardly do better than that.

What made his success even more memorable was the way various cities insisted on honouring him. Ephesus supplied a superbly decorated tent, Chios gave fodder for his horses and a vast number of animals for sacrifice, and the people of Lesbos gave him quantities of food and wine, so that he could entertain in real style.[6]

Writing about the Spartan king Demaratos, who was exiled and joined the Persians before Marathon, the historian Herodotos says:

His deeds were famous and the Spartans had always valued his opinion very highly. Moreover, he had added to Sparta's fame by winning the four-horse chariot race at Olympia, the only Spartan king ever to have done so.[7]

Note the way that last phrase is put: he does *not* say 'the only winner ever to have been a Spartan king'.

The expense of the whole business naturally made the owners careful over details. A *Manual of Horsemanship*, written shortly after 400 B.C., begins like this:

First, let me give you some advice to cut down your chances of being cheated when you go to buy a horse. Obviously, if a horse has not yet been broken in,

This bronze horse is from the treasures found at Zeus's temple at Olympia. Its rear hooves are missing, but otherwise it is complete in every detail.

it is the body you must look at; no one can get a clear idea of a horse's spirit until it has been ridden.

The first part of the body to look at is the feet. After all, a house would be no good if it was beautifully built but didn't have the necessary foundations. Just so, there would be no point having a warhorse which had a superb body but bad feet, because it wouldn't be able to make use of its good qualities. The first bit of the foot to look at is the hoof. Thick hooves are far better than thin ones, and you must also remember to note whether the horn of the hoof is curved up

This vase-painting shows an elegant young man on horseback. Part of the vase is missing, which is why there is a gap in the horse's front legs.

or down, at the front and back, or whether it is flush with the ground. High hooves have the soft central part, called the 'frog', further from the ground; with low ones, the weight is shared between the hardest and softest parts of the foot, as in the case of someone who has bandy legs.[8]

This manual is still regarded as a valuable guide to the horse and his ways.

After the choosing came the years of training, and finally the race itself:

The day for the chariot race arrived. Orestes was one of many competitors – one from Achaia, one from Sparta, two North Africans, Orestes himself fifth, then a man with chestnut colts from Aitolia, a Magnesian, a team of white horses from Ainia, one from Athens and one from Boiotia – ten altogether.

The officials drew lots to position the chariots, the trumpet sounded and they were off, the charioteers yelling and brandishing their reins. The whole stadium echoed with the clatter of wheels and the air was thick with dust as they raced along in a tight bunch, using their goads without mercy to get clear of the melée of hubs and snorting horses, while the wheels and the horses' backs were drenched in foam from the mouths of the teams which had overtaken them.

So far all the chariots were going well, but then at the turn from the sixth to the seventh lap the Ainian lost control of his horses and they ran headlong into one of the African chariots. A whole series of collisions followed and in a moment the course was a mass of wreckage. But the man from Athens, an expert charioteer, drew his team in to one side and waited, as his opponents drove on into the chaos, while Orestes all this time had been in last place, relying on a fast finish. When he saw that he had only one man to beat, Orestes gave a great shout and drove his horses on. At every turn he brought his left wheel right under the post, giving the outside horse its head while he held the inside one on a tight rein, and the two teams were soon neck and neck, with first one in the lead, then the other.

Now Orestes had only the last lap to run, and as he turned into it he slackened the left rein, just too soon. He hit the post, the hub of the wheel smashed across and he himself was thrown out of the chariot in a tangle of reins, and as he hit the ground the horses scattered all over the course. The crowd groaned in sympathy for him; after his other successes in the Games this was a terrible way to end. They watched, as he fell and was tossed head over heels in the air, until at last the other charioteers managed to stop his careering horses and cut him free. Not even his friends would have recognised the bloody corpse.[9]

This is still an exciting eye-witness report, even if you know that Orestes is really alive and well and living in Argos.

But the ordinary landowner would not have had the money for such things. More probably, his exercise would be hunting of some sort. A *Manual of Hunting*, from the same author as the one on horsemanship, has a section on pig-sticking:

If you go boar hunting you need dogs from India, Crete, Lokris or Sparta; also nets, javelins, spears and traps. Your dogs must be of the breeds I have mentioned, not just any sort, otherwise they won't dare to face their quarry. The nets should be the same as for hunting hares, but the javelins can be of any kind as long as their points are broad and razor-sharp and their shafts are

This band is from the vase shown on page 65. It shows Odysseus with Autolykos and his sons, hunting boar.

tough. The spears should have heads 1 metre long, and metal spikes sticking out from them; they should also be tough and the shaft as strong as that of any military spear. The traps are like those used for deer hunting.

The hunters should stay together, because this sport is tricky and demands teamwork. I will now tell you what everyone should do. First, when they are beating the area, they must have the dogs under control; I would send one of the Spartan bitches out on her own and keep the rest behind her. When she picks up the animal's tracks, follow her as closely as you can. If the ground is wet, there will be plenty of things to guide you; if it is dry, look for any signs of the undergrowth having been broken down or for tuskmarks on any of the trees. The bitch will probably end her tracking in some thick undergrowth; this is the sort of place where boars very often go to ground, because it is warm in winter and cool in summer. When the bitch reaches this spot, she will bark and, usually, the boar will stay where he is.[10]

As with the piece on boxing, Homer gives us an illustration of these techniques at work:

As dawn was breaking, they all started out for the hunt, Autolykos' sons, Odysseus and the pack of hounds. They went up through the steep woods of Mt Parnassos and soon found themselves in the windswept valleys above. The morning sun was just gilding the tops of the furrows when they came to a heavily wooded gully. In front ran the dogs, casting for the spoor, and then Autolykos' sons, and Odysseus, keeping close behind the pack and trying to get the feel of his long spear.

Flute-player. This time, although the girl is playing a double-flute, she is not moving about, and so has no need to fasten the flute round her head.

Their quarry was a huge boar, lying in a patch of dense brushwood, a spot completely sheltered from the wet blast of the winds, as well as from the sun and the rain, and thickly carpeted with leaves. The noise of men and dogs approaching reached him and he leapt up from his hiding-place, with back bristling and eyes flaming, and stood stock still, facing them. Odysseus, eager for the kill, was the first to move. With his spear poised in his strong hand, he rushed at the animal, but it was too quick for him; as he came on, it ran across his line of attack, giving him a long ugly gash above the knee, just missing the bone. Odysseus retaliated with a blow on its right shoulder and the spear-point went right through and came out the other side. The boar gave a scream and fell to the ground, mortally wounded. Autolykos' sons took charge of the body and carefully bandaged the wound Odysseus' daring had cost him. A magic charm helped to staunch the flow of blood and before long they were all back at Autolykos' palace.[11]

The Greeks loved their health and strength and thought old age was one of the gods' more cruel jokes, to be resisted as long as possible. But if their bodies weren't moving, then their tongues would be:

When Alkibiades began the final stage of his education, he was a fairly docile pupil, but he refused to play the flute. 'It is', he said, 'an activity fit only for the lower classes and slaves; a gentleman can play the lyre with a plectrum and still look like a gentleman, but once he starts blowing into a flute you can hardly recognise him. And another thing, a lyre leaves you free to talk or sing, but a flute blocks up your mouth completely. Leave the flute to the Thebans; they're such boring talkers anyway.'[12]

The Greek word for 'free time' (*schole*, pronounced 'skolleh') also meant conversation. The Athenians, in particular, had the gift of the gab and that is why their political system worked. It depended on the citizens standing up and speaking their mind in the Assembly, and altogether the Athenians seem to have got much more fun out of the business of politics than we do. Politics, festivals, plays, conversation, these were the things that occupied most of the Greeks' spare time. There are surprisingly few references to non-athletic games, such as dice or draughts. The next extract, again about Alkibiades, perhaps tells us more about him than about dice:

Achilles and Aias playing draughts. Their spears are kept handy in case the Trojans make a sudden attack.

Once, as quite a small boy, he was having a game of dice in a narrow street, and when it was his turn a loaded cart happened to come along. Alkibiades first told the driver to stop, as his dice had fallen in the way of the cart. The driver, being a rather grumpy sort of man, took no notice and drove straight on, faster. The other boys leapt out of the way, but Alkibiades threw himself flat on his face in front of the horses and told the driver to keep going if he wanted to. The fellow, in a panic, wrenched his horses to a standstill and all the passers-by screamed and rushed up to help.[12]

We have to do some detective work to get any idea of how these games were played. Alkibiades' game, played in a street, was probably fairly straightforward. In other sorts, you threw dice and moved pieces on a board, as in 'Ludo' or 'Snakes and Ladders'. They do seem to have played a game of pure skill, rather like draughts; for this, one of our pieces of information comes in a description of how Sokrates used to bamboozle his opponents in an argument (see Chapter 2):

As they are not experts in discussing things, you, Sokrates, can lead them on bit by bit with questions. Then, when all the questions are fitted together, they suddenly find they have gone quite wrong and are contradicting what they said at the beginning of the argument. It's rather like a novice playing an expert at draughts: he finds himself shut in and unable to move any of his pieces.[13]

One thing is certain: anybody who spent his life practising moves, as a modern chess champion has to, would have been looked on as a very queer fish. 'Don't go too far.'

On the question of how valuable athletics really were, agreement was not so complete. Here, to finish with, are the two sides of the argument, which was not confined to the ancient Greeks. Over 2,000 years later, one side of it was supported by the Duke of Wellington, who is supposed to have said, 'The battle of Waterloo was won on the playing-fields of Eton':

First, the main job of a soldier is to strike blows and avoid them; secondly, when there is hand-to-hand fighting he must be able to wrestle and up-end his opponent – they say that the Thebans beat the Spartans at Leuktra because they were trained in wrestling; thirdly, if his side loses he must be able to escape, and if they win he must be able to take his part in the pursuit.[14]

There are a thousand things wrong with Greece these days, but quite the worst nuisance of all are the athletes. They've no idea what life is all about and can't find out. When they're young, they're famous themselves and bring fame

The young man on the right has just won his contest, and is being presented with the victor's laurel-wreath.

to their city, but when they get old then they slop around like some old cloak with trailing ends.

I blame our habit of encouraging such useless pleasures and offering free meals as a reward. Wrestlers, sprinters, discus-throwers, boxers who can land you one right on the point of the jaw; was their victor's wreath ever a scrap of help to their city? Do any of them throw their discuses at the enemy or, as infantrymen, stand to repel the invaders of their homeland? Oh no, they've got more sense than to get mixed up in all that silly fighting. I say the olive wreaths ought to go to the real men, the sensible, honest men who do their best for the city; like the ones, perhaps, who frame peace-treaties and put an end to battles and revolutions. They do a good turn not just to the whole city but to the whole Greek world.[15]

7 · Gods, omens and oracles

Athene. She is here shown in her warlike pose, as guardian of Athens. Probably once the right hand held a spear, and the left a shield.

From time to time in every Greek city, when things were desperate or when there was particular reason for a celebration, a greater sacrifice than usual was made in honour of one of the gods:

They brought an ox in from the meadow, and everyone gathered round as the smith arrived with his anvil, and the bronze hammer and well-made tongs he used for handling gold. Athene, too, was at hand to accept the sacrifice.

The old charioteer Nestor gave the smith gold, and he softened it and wrapped it round the ox's horns, where its glitter would please the goddess most. Then, while two of them led the ox forward by its horns, Aretos came out of the store-room, carrying in one hand a flowered bowl of holy water, and in the other a basket of barley-grains. Thrasymedes stood nearby with a sharp axe, ready to sacrifice the victim, and Perseus held a bowl to catch its blood.

When everything was ready, Lord Nestor began the sacrifice. Holding the bowls of holy water and barley, he threw some of the ox's hair on the fire, and made a long prayer to Athene. Then, when the barley had been scattered, Thrasymedes struck the ox a mighty blow; his axe severed the tendons of its neck, and it collapsed on the ground. The watching women cried out; but the men held the ox's head while one of them cut its throat. Dark blood poured out, and life left the carcase.

At once they began cutting it up. First they removed slices from the thighs, and wrapped them in a double layer of fat, as custom demanded. Then they placed more meat on top, and old Nestor burned the whole lot on the fire, pouring red wine over it as it burned. The young men gathered round, holding five-pronged spits in their hands. When the thighs were all consumed and they'd tasted the entrails, they cut the rest of the carcase into small pieces, stuck them on the spits, and began roasting them over the flames.[1]

It may seem to us that the Greeks were sacrificing to beings that

Leading a bull to sacrifice.

didn't exist: omens, portents and cures like those described in this chapter can be explained in a perfectly natural way, without involving supernatural powers at all. The interesting thing is that many Greeks would have agreed with this view. Sokrates and his followers, in particular, were very sceptical about the existence of the gods. But they still carried on worshipping them. The stories and legends might be exaggerated or untrue, but that was no reason to abandon religion altogether. In much the same way, people today throw spilled salt over their shoulders, or avoid walking under ladders, without actually believing that they'll have bad luck if they don't.

This flexible, common-sense attitude to religion allowed the Greeks not only to make fun of the gods in a most un-English way (like the mockery of Dionysos in Chapter 5), but even to add or invent new ones when need arose. What separates their religion from most others is that even at its most solemn, it was still full of common sense, and often humour as well. The following story, for example, could be about no one else but Greeks:

The people of Andros were the first islanders the Athenians asked for money. When they refused to pay, the Athenians sent another message saying they'd no choice, as there were two very powerful gods in Athens, 'Please' and 'You'd better'. The Andrians, however, replied that at last they understood why Athens was so great and powerful: it was because they had two such fine gods to help them. There was nothing like that on Andros: the island was tiny and poverty-stricken, and the only gods they had were a useless pair called 'Flat broke' and 'Terribly sorry' — and it was because these gods refused to leave that the Andrians would never pay a penny, however much the Athenians tried to make them.[2]

The gods worshipped by the Greeks came from many different nations and countries. There were over fifty of them, and between them they looked after most of the problems of everyday life. Homer lists the most important. They lived on Mount Olympos, and were called the Olympians. Their names and principal functions are set out here.

Hermes. This portrait, by the famous sculptor Praxiteles, shows Hermes as the ideal of masculine beauty.

ZEUS The king of the gods. He controlled the weather, particularly thunder and lightning. He is the father of many of the other gods, and most of the greatest heroes of legendary times.

HERE Zeus's wife, the queen of the gods.

POSEIDON Zeus's brother, the god of the sea and of earthquakes.

DEMETER The earth-mother. She was the oldest of the gods, and looked after the earth and everything that grew in it.

APOLLO The god of music and poetry, hunting and prophecy. He was also responsible for causing and curing plagues and disease.

ATHENE Originally perhaps from Mycenae, she became the patron goddess of Athens. She was also the goddess of wisdom, logic and organisation.

HERMES The messenger-god. He was the patron god of travellers, and was associated with good luck. He guided the spirits of the dead down to the Underworld.

ARTEMIS The goddess of birth. Like her brother Apollo, she was also connected with hunting, but also dealt with witchcraft, magic and the moon.

APHRODITE The goddess of love and beauty, mother of Cupid (or Eros).

HEPHAISTOS The blacksmith-god, patron of artists and craftsmen.

HESTIA The goddess of hearth and home.

Above: *Artemis. This is an earlier
sculpture than the one shown on page v.*

Above right: *Apollo.*

Two important gods not among the Olympians were:

HADES King of the Underworld.
DIONYSOS The god of intoxication – wine, drugs, dancing. He soon became
  one of the most important of all the gods, and it was from his festivals that
  Greek drama began.

The Greeks had a simple, logical 'contract' with these gods – 'You

Aphrodite. The ideal of feminine beauty.

help us, and we'll look after you.' This idea dates back to primitive times, when natural disasters like thunderstorms and floods were thought to be controlled by gods, and special ceremonies were necessary to keep evil spirits at bay. Here, for example, is a 'good-weather ceremony' carried out by Jason and the Argonauts:

Deep in the wood they found an ancient, withered vine-stump, and cut it down to make a sacred image of the mountain goddess. Argos shaped it carefully, and they set it up on a rocky outcrop where it would be shaded by tall oaks, whose roots grow deeper than those of any other tree. Beside it they built an altar of small stones.

When everything was ready, they garlanded their heads with oak-leaves and began the ceremony, calling on the venerable Dindymian mother, whose home is in Phrygia, and on Titias and Kyllenos, the two Idean Daktyls from Crete whose job is to serve her and carry out her wishes. (These two were born in the Diktean cave, as their mother, the nymph Anchiale, held the earth of Oaxos in both hands.)

As he poured libations on the sacrificial flames, Jason prayed to the lady Mother to calm the storm-winds and send them away. Meanwhile, in time to Orpheus' music, the crew danced a high-stepping dance in full armour, clashing their swords and shields together to drown any ill-omened noise that might otherwise be heard.

The Lady Mother saw and smiled at their offering. She sent them an answer, clear signs of her favour. Ripe fruit fell from the trees, and the earth sent up lush grass of its own accord, covered with flowers. Wild beasts left their lairs on the mountain and came up to them, wagging their tails and nuzzling the Argonauts' hands.

But the last sign was the greatest of all. Up to now there had been no fresh water on Mount Didymon; but now, without need of digging, a clear spring appeared and flowed down from the summit. It has never dried up to this day, and the people there call it Jason's spring.

When the sacrifice was over they held a great feast on the Hill of Bears in the Lady Mother's honour, singing hymns to all-powerful Rheia. By dawn the next day the winds had gone, and they were able to leave the island without difficulty.[3]

By the fifth century B.C., when men were beginning to question the whole relationship between man and god, ceremonies like that were reserved for important occasions. For everyday purposes a simple offering would be enough. In the following account of a healing at Asklepios' temple, all the worshippers have to do is leave the god an offering and spend the night in his temple:

We left home, the old man and I, and went to the temple as quickly as we could. The altar by Hephaistos' holy fire was covered with offerings: rice-cakes and unleavened bread, the usual sort of thing. I put the old man to bed, the way they tell you; then we all tucked ourselves up for the night. There were hundreds of people there, suffering from all sorts of different diseases. The attendant put the lights out, and told us to go to sleep, and not to move about, whatever strange noises we heard. We lay there in orderly rows for a long time. Then suddenly I noticed a priest going round the holy tables gathering up all the bread and fish people had left there. Then he went to the altar, and consecrated the offerings – into a knapsack he had with him.

Nothing happened after that for a while. Then the god appeared with his attendants, and started his rounds, examining all the patients to see what was wrong with them. His attendants followed, carrying a pestle and mortar, and a medicine chest.

The first person he dealt with had styes on his eyes. The god mixed up a poultice of garlic, syrup of figs, mastic-gum and vinegar. Then he lifted up the man's eyelids and plastered it all over them. God, it must have stung! Next he came to my old man, and sat down beside him. First he wiped his eyes with a cloth, and told one of the attendants to cover his face with a purple towel. Then Asklepios began whistling softly – and two gigantic snakes came gliding out from behind the altar.

They disappeared under the purple towel and began licking the old man's eyelids – or so it appeared to me. And before you could drink a cup of wine, the old man got up – and he could see! I was so pleased I started clapping and shouting; and immediately the god and the snakes disappeared. All the sick people got up and began shaking the old fellow's hand and congratulating him. I went out; I wanted to make a thank-offering to the god for helping my poor old friend.[4]

The light, mocking tone of this passage – which is from a comedy – is probably nearer to the truth of Greek religious feeling than the awesome, dark magnificence of the gods in tragedy (page 82, for example). To the Greeks their gods were men – gigantic men with supernatural powers, but subject to love, anger, hate and despair just like anyone else. When Aphrodite tries to take part in a battle outside Troy, she is wounded by one of the Greek heroes, and runs sobbing back to her father Zeus. Other gods, it is true, do make more spectacular personal appearances:

Poseidon strode off down the rocky mountainside, and the woods and ridges

Poseidon. The head of this statue is shown on page ii. Originally the right hand held a trident, poised for throwing.

trembled at his immortal step. His journey took three strides; on the fourth he reached his destination: Aigai, the shimmering site of his everlasting golden palace under the sea. There he yoked a pair of swift horses to his chariot: magnificent beasts with bronze-clad feet and golden manes that streamed in the wind. Then the god put on his own golden robes, picked up a fine golden whip, climbed into his chariot and drove out across the waves. All the sea-creatures recognised their king, and gambolled at his feet; and the sea itself parted for him, so that the bronze axle of his chariot was not even damp as the leaping horses bore him along to the Achaian fleet.[5]

But usually the gods avoid appearing on earth in a recognisable form. They transmit their messages to men in the form of omens – making sure first that there is a prophet at hand to explain them. Sometimes the omens were very bad, like this one sent to Teiresias in Sophokles' *Antigone*:

I was in my ancient prophetic seat,
Where the birds gather to give me omens,
When all at once I heard their voices –
A strange, maddened screaming, as they tore
Each other with their talons, beating their wings
In a message not hard to understand.
I was frightened, and went to sacrifice.
The fire was laid ready on the altar,
But when I tried to light it, it would not burn –
Instead, a hideous liquid mess oozed out
Over the ashes, hissing and spluttering;
The gall-bladder burst, and the fat melted
And dripped from the naked thighs. These are clear
Omens from heaven, and we must heed them.[6]

At other times the messages sent by the gods are exciting and vivid, and need a great deal of explanation. Here is Odysseus' description of what happened while the Greek fleet was gathering at Aulis, ready for the Trojan War:

We were making a sacrifice to the gods, on an altar set up in the shade of a splendid plane-tree, beside a stream of clear water, when all at once we saw an amazing sight. A huge snake, with blood-red markings on its back, a monster sent by Olympian Zeus himself, appeared from behind the altar and moved swiftly towards the plane-tree. On one of the upper branches there was a brood of nine sparrows: a mother and her eight unfledged chicks, cowering among the leaves. The snake first ate the babies, for all their piteous cheeping; then, as the mother fluttered to and fro, grieving for her lost children, he snatched her by one wing and devoured her too.

So mother and babies were eaten. But now Zeus, son of wily Kronos, made the omen even more remarkable: for he turned the snake to stone before our eyes. We stood amazed by this omen from heaven, until Kalchas explained it to us. 'Long-haired Achaians,' he said, 'why are you amazed? Zeus the Counsellor has sent us the sign we have been waiting for, an omen which will not be fulfilled for many years, but which men will remember for ever. Those nine sparrows, the mother and her eight babies, are the nine years we shall spend besieging Troy with its wide streets; for we shall not capture it until ten years from now.' That was what he said; and now everything is being accomplished.[7]

But the gods did not always oblige by providing omens like these. In that case they had to be persuaded into doing so, and so over the years a process was evolved which, although it sounds unlikely to us, satisfied most Greeks, at least until the arrival of Sokrates (see Chapter 2). This process was to consult an 'oracle' – a sort of information centre where you asked your question and the god, usually Zeus or Apollo, gave you his answer. Of course, he wouldn't do this direct. The earliest oracle, of Zeus at Dodona in north-west Greece, gave answers through the rustling of leaves in an oak tree. As Plato said:

People in those days, being rather more naive than they are now, were quite happy to believe oak-trees and rocks, so long as the answers were right.[8]

But for centuries after this the most important oracle was that of Apollo at Delphi. Why important? Presumably because 'the answers were right'. At this oracle you were ushered into a dark room and put your question to the priestess, who sat, heavily drugged, and waited for inspiration from Apollo. The answers came through her in verse and were written down by the attendant priests. This does sound slightly more trustworthy than the oak-leaf method, but it is not surprising that some people wanted proof that it *was* a reliable method:

Now that Kyros had taken over the Persian empire from Astyages and was beginning to expand it, Kroisos decided that, if at all possible, he should try and control the Persians before they got out of hand. So he made arrangements to consult oracles in both Greece and Libya, and sent messengers off to Delphi, to Abai in Phokis, to Dodona, to the oracles of Amphiareus and Trophonios

The remains of Apollo's temple at Delphi, seen from the theatre. (See also next page, and page 134.)

and to Branchidai in Milesia. Apart from all these Greek ones, he also tried the oracle of Ammon in Libya. His idea was to find out first how well-informed they were; then, if their information turned out to be accurate, he would send a second deputation, to ask whether he should attack Persia.

The Lydians he chose for this mission duly set off for the different oracles.

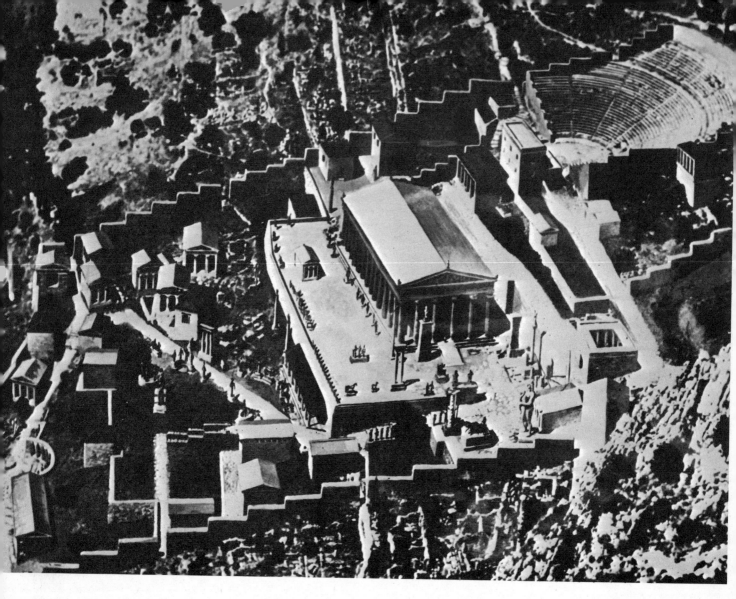

This reconstruction shows Apollo's magnificent shrine at Delphi, as it probably was in its heyday. The walk up the mountainside continues until it reaches the stadium shown on page 26.

Their instructions were to wait 100 days from the date of their departure and then ask the oracle what Kroisos, king of Lydia, was doing at that very moment; and they were to bring the written answers back to him in Sardis. No one knows what the rest of the oracles said, but at Delphi, as soon as the envoys reached the inner room of the temple to ask their question, the Priestess gave forth the following verses:

I know the number of the grains of sand;
I know the compass of the sea. I hear
And understand the voices of the dumb,
Although their speech is silent. Now I sense
The smell of a tortoise in its stony shell,
Boiling with lamb's flesh in a pot of bronze,
And under it is bronze, and bronze above.

The envoys wrote this down and went back to Sardis.

When all the other replies had come in, Kroisos opened each document in turn and read it. All of them left him quite unmoved, except the one from Delphi. As soon as he read this one, he began to offer up prayers of thanksgiving and declared that the Delphic oracle was the only real one, because it had found out what he'd been doing. When all the envoys had left on their journeys, he had kept carefully to the timetable and then made his experiment, which involved about the most unlikely activity anybody could think of: with his own hands, he had chopped up a tortoise and a lamb into bits and stewed them in a bronze cauldron which had a bronze lid.[9]

Kroisos' experiment was surely fool-proof – and so, unless there was a leakage of information, the Priestess must have had second sight. At any rate, Kroisos was convinced, and sent a second deputation to Delphi and also to the oracle of Amphiareus, some 112 km to the east of Delphi. Although we don't know what the answer from here had been, it must have been near enough for Kroisos to think the oracle worth trying again, if only as a cross-check on Delphi. The envoys asked both oracles the same two questions:

'Kroisos, king of Lydia and her empire, believing these two oracles to be the only real ones on earth, has sent you gifts worthy of your great powers; he now asks you, should he invade Persia, and should he try to find an ally?'

The two oracles gave these questions identical answers: they forecast that if Kroisos invaded Persia he would destroy a great empire, and advised him to find out which Greek state was the strongest and make an alliance with it.

When the answers reached Kroisos he was delighted, and quite confident that he would soon put an end to the empire of Kyros.[10]

Unfortunately for Kroisos, the great empire he destroyed was his own. When oracles spoke as cleverly as this – and they often did – it was impossible to prove them wrong. But sometimes they *did* come down firmly on one side of the fence:

Alexander told his commanders to take over and left on the long journey to Ammon. It was not only long but very hard going, with two particular dangers: lack of water, because the journey takes several days through the Libyan desert, and the possibility of sand-storms blowing up from the interior. Practically everyone realised how dangerous it was, but once Alexander had made up his mind to do something, it was a hard job for anyone else to change it.

But they managed to cross the desert, and as soon as Alexander reached the temple, the priest of Ammon delivered to him the greetings of the god, as though they came from Alexander's own father. Alexander asked whether any of his father's murderers had escaped his hands, but when the priest begged him not to say such things, as his father was no ordinary mortal, he rephrased the question and asked whether all Philip's murderers had been punished; he also asked whether he would become ruler of the world. The oracle assured him that he would and that Philip's murder had been fully avenged, in return for which information Alexander presented the god with a number of magnificent presents, and gave the priests a handsome tip.[11]

Clearly, now that Alexander was master of Greece and more besides, there was no point in upsetting him. The fact that Ammon was so hard to get to may have helped to give the place an air of mystery. Delphi, set in a very different type of scenery, can still today make you feel it is a magic place.

But magic or not, even here things sometimes went wrong:

What happened then to the priestess of Apollo? She went down to her prophetic seat, they say, very slowly and unwillingly. It was clear, as soon as the first questions were asked, that the spirit was too strong for her, almost as if she was some ship driven by a hurricane; her voice was harsh and she was raving, apparently under the spell of some evil demon. Finally her madness reached a climax, and with a ghastly scream she rushed for the door and hurled herself outside. Everyone else ran for another door, not only the questioners, but Nikandros the priest and all the temple attendants who were there. A little later they came back and picked her up, still raving. She lived, but only for a few days.[12]

Barring accidents like this, perhaps the most memorable oracle you could have consulted was the one of Trophonios at Lebadea, about 30 km east of Delphi. This one, you may remember, did not pass Kroisos' test. This is what it was like to 'visit Trophonios':

When you want to go down to the oracle, you spend a number of days in a special building, which is sacred to the Good Spirit and Good Luck. While you are there, you are not allowed to have a hot bath; you can only have one in the river Herkyna. And you get plenty of meat from the sacrifices. A diviner is present at all these to inspect the entrails, after which he tells you whether Trophonios is going to give you a friendly reception. If the signs are good, you descend like this. First, two citizen's sons, about thirteen years old, take you to the river Herkyna. They smear you with oil and wash you, and after this you are taken by the priests, not straight to the oracle, but to two springs of water which are very close to each other. Here you have to drink the water of Forgetfulness, so that you forget everything you have been thinking about so far; then you drink the water of Memory, so that you can remember what you see as you descend.

Then you see a statue, which they say was made by Daidalos. You pray to this, and then proceed to the oracle, wearing a linen tunic covered with ribbons, and country boots on your feet. The oracle is on the mountain, beyond the group of trees, and round it is a circular pavement of white marble, the size of a small threshing-floor and just over 1 metre high. In this are fixed bronze spikes, held together by crossbars of the same metal, and between them doors have been fitted. Inside all this is a hole in the earth, man-made and very cleverly done. I would say it was about 2 metres in diameter and no more than 4 metres deep.

There is no way of getting down into it, but the attendants bring you a thin, rather shaky ladder. When you get down, you find a gap between the floor and the constructed part, 40 cm wide and 20 cm high. You lie face upwards, holding in your hands barley-cakes mixed with honey, and push yourself into the hole feet first, trying hard to get your knees to go through. Once these *have* got through, the rest of you is sucked in quickly, just as the current in a large, fast-flowing river will catch you and pull you under.

After this, you learn what is going to happen in the future. Not everybody is instructed in the same way; some see the future, others hear it. You return by the same route, coming out feet first. Nobody – they say – has ever been killed in the descent except one of Demetrios' bodyguard; but apparently he

The navel-stone at Delphi. This was one of the most sacred objects in the shrine. It was believed to mark the exact centre of the world.

didn't go through any of the usual ceremonies beforehand and went down not to consult the god, but with the idea of stealing the gold and silver from the shrine.

When you reappear from the cave, you are again taken by the priests to the chair of Memory, which is quite near the shrine, and when you have sat down they ask you about everything you have seen or heard. Then they hand you over to your friends, who lift you up and take you back to the building sacred to the Good Spirit and Good Luck; because by this time you are paralysed with terror and unconscious of yourself and everybody round you. Later, though, you regain consciousness and can even laugh again.[13]

Nowadays we say to someone who looks gloomy: 'Have you lost something?' In Greek times they said: 'Been to see Trophonios, have you?'

The authority of the Delphic oracle was still complete at the time of the battle of Marathon (490 B.C.), but as the century went on it began to be doubted more and more. Of course, there were still some people who believed in it, mainly the older people, some of whom held important positions in the cities. Sokrates, on trial before such people for corrupting the young men of Athens, said in his defence:

Gentlemen, please do not interrupt even if I seem to be exaggerating, because the words that I'm going to repeat to you are not my own but those of the highest authority: I call as my next witness – the Delphic oracle.

Now, you know Chairephon. Well, one day he went to Delphi and very bravely asked the oracle a question – now please, gentlemen, listen to me – he asked whether there was anybody wiser than me. The priestess said: 'Nobody'. Now when I heard this I wondered: 'What does Apollo really mean, behind this riddle? I know I'm not a wise man in any sense of the word, so why does he say I'm the wisest of all men? Surely Apollo can't be lying: that wouldn't be right.'

I was puzzled for some time, but then, with some reluctance, I decided to prove the matter one way or the other. I interviewed one of our so-called 'wisest' men, because I thought that the only way to correct Apollo's mistake was to be able to go to the oracle and point out: 'You said I was the wisest man of all, but this fellow is wiser.' So I interviewed this person – no names, gentlemen – and I came to the conclusion that although many people, including himself, were convinced that he was wise, in fact he wasn't.

In this vase-painting, a priestess is shown making a prophecy.

Euripides — one of the first agnostics. His unpopular beliefs led to his banishment, and eventual death in exile.

Then I went to someone who was even more highly thought of, with the same result. From there I went on to interview a whole succession of people, and although I realised that I was becoming unpopular, which made me very sad, I felt that I must do my religious duty as thoroughly as possible: to find out what Apollo meant, I had to question everyone who was thought to be wise.

As a result of this enquiry, I have had to put up with the most hostile and unpleasant remarks. But the real answer is that God is wise, and what the oracle meant was that the wisdom of man is really quite worthless. Apollo was using my name as an example, and what he was saying was: 'The wisest man is the one like Sokrates, who realises that as far as wisdom goes he is a non-starter.'[14]

In the Athens of the late fifth century, it was still safest to put your doubts into the mouths of actors. In Euripides' *Elektra* we find a discussion of the very point made by Sokrates in the last extract: 'Surely Apollo can't be lying — that wouldn't be right.' Orestes has been ordered by Apollo to return from exile and kill his mother and her lover Aigisthos, because they murdered his father Agamemnon. His sister (Elektra) urges him on to do the deed:

Apollo, the all-seeing. Here again he is shown as the ideal of masculine beauty.

ORESTES What shall we do to our mother, then? Kill her?

ELEKTRA Don't tell me that the sight of your mother's face has made you sorry for her?

ORESTES But how, how can I kill the woman who bore me and brought me up?

ELEKTRA In the same way that she killed your father and mine.

ORESTES That was a stupid answer of Apollo's . . .

ELEKTRA Well, if Apollo is stupid, who is wise?

ORESTES . . . telling me to murder her. It is a crime.

ELEKTRA To avenge your father's death?

ORESTES As yet I am an innocent man, but if I killed her I would be a criminal, a hunted man.

ELEKTRA You would be a poor son not to defend your father's memory.

ORESTES Perhaps it wasn't really Apollo? Perhaps some evil spirit was impersonating him?

ELEKTRA Sitting on his holy seat? I hardly think so.

ORESTES And I hardly think that his answer was a good one.

ELEKTRA This is no time for you to be a coward. No, you must lure her into the trap, as Aigisthos helped her to do to her husband.

ORESTES Very well. A terrible risk, a terrible deed – if this is what the gods want, it shall be done. But it is not an exploit that brings me any joy.[15]

By the time of Alexander (late fourth century B.C.) the great days of oracles were over. His visit to Ammon was probably more a piece of propaganda than an act of religious faith. Even so, they went on being consulted for centuries; the last recorded words from Delphi came in reply to the Roman Emperor Julian, as late as A.D. 363:

Go, tell the prince: the sculptured temple lies
Ruined on the ground; no grove is left,
No sacred laurel tree; the fountain
Is silent, and the once-fair stream run dry.[16]

Chronological Chart

CENTURY	AUTHORS AND PRINCIPAL WORKS c. = approximate date	DATE	IMPORTANT HISTORICAL EVENTS c. = approximate date
B.C. 4000–1000		B.C. 3400–1600 1600–1200 c. 1184	Early Minoan civilisation in Crete Late Minoan civilisation in Crete and Mycenae Troy captured by Greeks after 10-year siege
899–800	HOMER – nothing whatever known about his personal life. Works include *Iliad* (epic poem about part of Trojan War), *Odyssey* (epic poem about wanderings of Odysseus).		
799–700	HESIOD – not much known about his personal life. Works include *Theogony* (poem about early gods of Greece), *Works and Days* (poetic manual on farming and farm life).	776 753	First Olympic Games Foundation of Rome
699–600	ALKAIOS (c. 630–560) wrote short poems on love, war, the gods, banquets, etc.		*Persian Empire begins to grow*
599–500	PYTHAGORAS (c. 580–20) – a philosopher who wrote books about mathematics, music, astronomy and the after-life. AISCHYLOS (525–456) – wrote tragedies; 7 survive, including *The Persians*, *Prometheus Bound* and *The Oresteia*.	560–546	Kroisos king of Lydia *Persian expansion continues* *Greek states like Athens and Sparta grow in power*
499–400	SOPHOKLES (495–06) – wrote tragedies; 7 survive, including *Oedipus the King* and *Antigone*. ZENO (495–35) – wrote on mathematical problems. HERODOTOS (c. 480–25) – wrote a history of the rise and fall of the Persian Empire. EURIPIDES (480–06) – wrote tragedies; 19 survive, including *The Bacchae*, *Medea* and *Alkestis*.	499 490 480 479 431 415 404	Persians first attack Greek cities Battle of Marathon Battle of Salamis; Battle of Thermopylae Battle of Plataia – Persians finally defeated *Great period of Athenian history, part of it under leadership of Perikles* War between Athens and Sparta begins Athenian expedition to Sicily (destroyed 413) Final defeat of Athens

SOKRATES (469–399) – a philosopher. Wrote nothing himself, but see *Plato* and *Xenophon*.

THUCYDIDES (460–400) – wrote a history of the war between Athens and Sparta.

HIPPOKRATES (c. 460–400) – wrote various books on medicine.

ARISTOPHANES (c. 448–380) – wrote comedies; 11 survive, including *Peace*, *The Frogs*, *The Birds*.

XENOPHON (c. 430–355) – wrote books on history and philosophy; many of his works are about Sokrates.

PLATO (427–348) – wrote books on philosophy, mainly about Sokrates' teaching.

371 — Battle of Leuktra; Thebes ends Spartan leadership in Greece.

359 — Philip becomes king of Macedon; expansion begins of Macedonian power in Greece.

338 — Philip defeats Greeks at Battle of Chaironea.

336 — Alexander the Great becomes king of Macedon; expansion begins towards east.

331 — Alexandria founded (by Alexander). Contained a huge library, and a lighthouse that was one of the seven wonders of the world.

323 — Death of Alexander the Great

Throughout this century the power of Rome is growing

399–300

ARISTOTLE (384–22) – wrote notebooks mainly on philosophy and science.

DEMOSTHENES (383–22) – wrote speeches on legal matters and politics.

THEOPHRASTOS (c. 371–287) – wrote books on philosophy and botany, including *Characters*.

MENANDER (343–292) – wrote comedies, of which 1 survives complete, plus fragments of over 100 others.

EUCLID (c. 330–260) – wrote a treatise on geometry.

299–200

APOLLONIOS (c. 295–15) – wrote *The Voyage of Argo*, epic poem in imitation of Homer, describing Jason's search for the Golden Fleece.

Continued growth of Rome and stagnation in Greece

199–0

POLYBIOS (c. 202–120) – wrote history books, of which 4 survive.

136 — Roman conquest of Greece ends with capture of Corinth. Greece becomes a Roman satellite.

A.D.

1–200

PLUTARCH (c. 46–120) – wrote 50 short biographies of famous historical figures, including *Alexander*. Also, 83 essays on science, religion and life in general.

ARRIAN (95–175) – wrote a biography of Alexander the Great.

PAUSANIAS (c. 140–210) – wrote a guidebook to Greece.

Suggestions for further reading

1. Authors quoted in this book

Aischylos, 7 plays, translated by Vellacott (Penguin Classics, 2 vols).
Alkaios, Fragments, with trans. (Loeb library, Macmillan).
Apollonios, *Voyage of Argo*, trans. by Rieu (Penguin Classics).
Aristophanes, Complete plays, trans. by various hands (Bantam Classics).
    Acharnians, *Peace*, trans. by McLeish (*Four Greek Plays*, Longman).
    The Birds, *The Frogs*, trans. by McLeish (*The Frogs* etc, Longman).
Aristotle, Complete works (Loeb library).
Arrian, *Campaigns of Alexander* (Penguin Classics).
Demosthenes, Complete works (Loeb library).
Euripides, 10 plays, trans. by Vellacott (Penguin Classics, 3 vols).
    4 plays, trans. by various hands (Dell paperbacks).
    Medea, trans. by McLeish (*The Frogs and Other Greek Plays*, Longman).
Homer, *The Iliad*, trans. by Rieu (Penguin Classics).
    The Odyssey, trans. by Rieu (Penguin Classics).
Herodotos, *Histories*, trans. by de Selincourt (Penguin Classics).
Hesiod, Works (Loeb library).
Pausanias, *Guide to Greece* (Penguin Classics, 2 vols).
Plato, *The Last Days of Socrates* (Penguin Classics).
    Meno and Protagoras (Penguin Classics).
Plutarch, *Rise and Fall of Athens* (Penguin Classics).
    Moralia (Loeb library and Penguin Classics).
    Life of Alexander, in *Lives* (Loeb library).
Polybios, *Histories* (Loeb library).
Pseudo-Xenophon, *The Constitution of Athens* (Loeb library: The Old Oligarch).
Sophokles, 7 plays, trans. by Watling (Penguin Classics, 2 vols).
    Oedipus the King and Antigone, trans. by McLeish (*Four Greek Plays*, Longman).

Theophrastos, *Characters*, trans. by Vellacott (Penguin Classics).
Thukydides, *Peloponnesian War*, trans. by Warner (Penguin Classics).
Xenophon, Selected works, trans. by various hands (Penguin Classics, 3 vols).

2. General reading

P. D. Arnott, *Introduction to the Greek World* (Macmillan).
   A good general introduction, relating Ancient Greece to what is left today.
R. W. Livingstone (ed.), *The Pageant of Greece* (O.U.P.).
   Text and pictures showing the heritage of the Greeks.
P. Mackendrick, *The Greek Stones Speak* (Methuen).
   A survey, superbly illustrated, of all the important archaeological discoveries
   made in Greece and Asia Minor.
J. Maclean-Todd, *Voices from the Past* (Macmillan).
   An anthology containing the best bits of almost every Greek and Latin
   author of importance, in usually very good translations.
K. McLeish (ed.), *Aspects of Greek Life Series* (Longman).
   Six short books on various aspects of Greek life: Theatre, Mycenae, Ships,
   Gods, etc.
H. J. Rose, *A Handbook of Greek Mythology* (Methuen).
   Versions of the better-known Greek myths, both as dealt with in literature
   and according to archaeology and anthropology.
H. H. Scullard and Van Der Heyden, *Atlas of the Classical World* (Nelson).
   A truly superb book: 500 photos, maps, diagrams, and a good text.
D. E. Strong, *The Classical World* (Hamlyn).
   A picture-book, full of beautiful photos.

List of passages quoted

1 · War

[1] Homer, *Iliad* XI, 67–121 with cuts
[2] Thukydides I, 11
[3] Herodotos VI, 111–17
[4] Herodotos VII, 208–12
[5] Thukydides IV, 40
[6] Tyrtaios, *Ox. Book of Gk. Verse*, 98
[7] Polybios XVIII, 29–30
[8] Arrian I, 6
[9] Plutarch, *Alexander*, 16
[10] Arrian VI, 9–10, 13
[11] Homer, *Iliad* III, 328–82
[12] Archilochos, *Ox. Book of Gk. Verse*, 104
[13] Homer, *Iliad* XXII, 395–404
[14] Herodotos IX, 78–9
[15] Homer, *Iliad* XXII, 437–72
[16] Simonides, *Ox. Book of Gk. Verse*, 212

2 · The enquiring mind

[1] Aischines, *Timarchos*, 11–12
[2] Aristotle, *Politics*, 1337b 23–9, 1338a 13–22, 28–30
[3] Thukydides V, 69–70
[4] Plutarch, *Lykurgos*, 22
[5] Plato, *Protagoras*, 325 C–6A, 326C–D
[6] Aristophanes, *Frogs*, 1083–98
[7] Xenophon, *Symposion* III, 5
[8] Demosthenes, *de Corona*, 199f
[9] Plutarch, *Demosthenes*, 7, 11
[10] Plutarch, *Lysander*, 15, incorporating Euripides, *Elektra*, 167–83
[11] Plutarch, *Themistokles*, 11
[12] Plutarch, *Themistokles*, 18
[13] Plutarch, *de Liberis Educandis*, 13
[14] Plato, *Meno*, 71C–3A
[15] Plato, *Meno*, 78B–9A
[16] Plato, *Meno*, 80A
[17] Aristotle, *Historia Animalium*, 534A 12–19, 29–32
[18] Hippokrates, *Epidemics* I, 23
[19] Quoted from Dell's *History of Maths*, 1922
[20] Plutarch, *VII Sacrum Convivium* I, 147

3 · Ships and the sea

[1] Homer, *Odyssey* V, 228–61
[2] Homer, *Odyssey* V, 264–7
[3] Apollonios, *Argonautica* I, 363–93
[4] Homer, *Odyssey* XIII, 70–9, 81–7
[5] Apollonios, *Argonautica* II, 549–603
[6] Aischylos, *Agamemnon*, 650–60
[7] Demosthenes, *in Zenothemin*, 4–9
[8] Herodotos IV, 42
[9] Thukydides VI, 31–2
[10] Aischylos, *Persians*, 355–432
[11] Herodotos VIII, 86
[12] Thukydides VII, 36
[13] Thukydides VII, 70–2
[14] Hesiod, *Works and Days*, 618–30

4 · Everyday life

[1] Loeb, Select Papyri II, 136
[2] Greek Historical Inscriptions, 79A 34–49
[3] Pseudo-Xenophon I, 10
[4] Demosthenes, *in Meidian*, 47
[5] Herodotos VIII, 75
[6] Homer, *Odyssey* XX, 147–63
[7] Homer, *Odyssey* X, 348–67, 371–3
[8] Homer, *Odyssey* VI, 86–100
[9] Aristophanes, *Peace*, 1140–58
[10] Homer, *Iliad* XI, 628–41
[11] Homer, *Odyssey* I, 136–43
[12] Homer, *Odyssey* VIII, 256–65
[13] Alkaios, Lobel & Page edition, frag. Z22
[14] Herodotos VI, 126–9

⁵ Demosthenes, *in Aristokraten*, 207
⁶ Xenophon, *Oikonomikos* IX, 2–4, 6–10
⁷ Theophrastos, *Characters* X and XVI
⁸ Thukydides II, 40

5 · The theatre

¹ Euripides, *Bacchae*, 64–88
² Aristophanes, *Peace*, 774–818
³ Aristophanes, *Frogs*, 460–86
⁴ Sophokles, *Antigone*, 441–89, 497–525
⁵ Euripides, *Bacchae*, 1043–152 with cuts
⁶ Euripides, *Bacchae*, 1389–92
⁷ Aristophanes, *Clouds*, 133–258 with cuts
⁸ Euripides, *Medea*, 364–400

⁹ Euripides, *Medea*, 1293–419
¹⁰ Aristophanes, *Peace*, 1–81

6 · Time off

¹ Homer, *Iliad* XXIII, 740–2, 750–60, 763–83
² Polybios V, 73.10
³ Plato, *Laws*, 830A–B
⁴ Homer, *Iliad* XXIII, 653–99
⁵ Homer, *Iliad* XXIII, 826–49
⁶ Plutarch, *Alkibiades*, 11–12
⁷ Herodotos VI, 70
⁸ Xenophon, *de Re Equestri* I, 1–3
⁹ Sophokles, *Elektra*, 698–756
¹⁰ Xenophon, *de Venatione* X, 1–7
¹¹ Homer, *Odyssey* XIX, 428–58
¹² Plutarch, *Alkibiades* II, 2–3, 4–5
¹³ Plato, *Republic*, 487B–C
¹⁴ Plutarch, *Symposion* II, 5 (= *Moralia* 639F)
¹⁵ Euripides frag 284, 1–4, 10–28

7 · Gods, omens and oracles

¹ Homer, *Odyssey* III, 430–63
² Herodotos VIII, 111
³ Apollonios, *Argonautica* I, 1117–52
⁴ Aristophanes, *Wealth*, 653–747 with cuts
⁵ Homer, *Iliad* XIII, 17–31
⁶ Sophokles, *Antigone*, 999–1013
⁷ Homer, *Iliad* II, 305–330
⁸ Plato, *Phaidros* 275B
⁹ Herodotos I, 46–48
¹⁰ Herodotos I, 53–54
¹¹ Plutarch, *Alexander*, 26–7
¹² Plutarch, *de Defectu Oraculorum* 438 B–C
¹³ Pausanias IX, 4–5
¹⁴ Plato, *Apology*, 20E–21E, 23A–B
¹⁵ Euripides, *Elektra*, 967–87
¹⁶ Cedrenus (ed. Bekker I page 532/304A)

Ruins of the tholos, *or circular shrine,*
at Delphi.